Yearning

Living Between How It Is
& How It Ought to Be

M. Craig Barnes

Foreword by
Martin E. Marty

INTERVARSITY PRESS
DOWNERS GROVE, ILLINOIS 60515

InterVarsity Press is the book-publishing division of InterVarsity Christian Fellowship, a student movement active on campus at hundreds of universities, colleges and schools of nursing in the United States of America, and a member movement of the International Fellowship of Evangelical Students. For information about local and regional activities, write Public Relations Dept., InterVarsity Christian Fellowship, 6400 Schroeder Rd., P.O. Box 7895, Madison, WI 53707-7895.

All Scripture quotations, unless otherwise indicated, are from the Holy Bible, New International Version. Copyright © 1973, 1978, International Bible Society. Used by permission of Zondervan Bible Publishers.

Cover illustration: Donna Nelson

ISBN 0-8308-1378-0

Printed in the United States of America

Library of Congress Cataloging-in-Publication Data

Barnes, M. Craig
    Yearning: living between how it is & how it ought to be/M. Craig
Barnes.
      p. cm.
    Includes bibliographical references.
    ISBN 0-8308-1378-0
    1. Christian life—1960-   2. Barnes, M. Craig I. Title.
    BV4501.2.B38286   1992
248.4—dc20   91-30416
                                                          CIP

17	16	15	14	13	12	11	10	9	8	7	6	5	4	3	2	1
04	03	02	01	00	99	98	97	96	95	94	93	92	91			

To the people of Christ Presbyterian Church,
earthen vessels I have come to love and treasure

Foreword

Best-seller lists are full of books by physicians who, writing out of their experience with illness and health, provide readers with graphic and useful material for improving their physical well-being. Those who aspire to rise in the world of business like to read books by high-achieving executives, books with titles that begin with the words "How to. . . ." Books by lawyers throw light on paths made tangled by a litigious society, paths full of opportunity for those who want to make their living in law or to avoid trouble with it.

Doctors, business people and lawyers have come to be the exemplars—in medieval times they would have been called "exempla," models and molds—for vast lay audiences in our time. Pastors, however, represent a profession whose gifts most people overlook. When they write in the context of their calling, basing their work on what they experience and observe, they do not have an automatic audience, a readership poised to take in what they write. Those who come across this book by Craig Barnes can begin to see what they've been missing if they have overlooked what ministers of congregations have to pass on to them.

Oh, I have no doubt that ministers—by which I mean officially credentialed and ordained professionals—read each other just as they watch each other. They too seek health and achievement and walk tangled paths, and therefore find it profitable to read books about or by notable fellow professionals. It's hard to picture any of them who would not find much of value in these pages, as they compare their lives with that of Barnes, their congregations with the one he serves in Madison, Wisconsin.

This book, however, is for *all* kinds of ministers, which includes the people we usually call the laity. They have to seek health and achievement and walk paths in the most arduous of all vocations: the simple living of their ordinary lives. Books by doctors, business leaders or lawyers can help them when medical, executive or legal matters confront them. But who deals with what it is that they must do to make sense of a world that is broken and remains so, of promises that even God does not always seem to keep? Answer: not many, or not many capably.

Why, one might ask, is the genre of books on living by Christian ministers so often overlooked, even by Christians? My hunch is that many pastors do not know how to employ their experiences as exempla for others, at least not without turning preachy along the way. Another explanation is an obvious one that will dawn on anyone who reads the chapters that follow: few of them have time or find time to do the writing. Craig Barnes does not have the time, but he made some.

The foremost reason for the paucity of effective books like this one, I suspect, has to do with institutions and culture. For reasons too complex to go into here, Christian congregations have to, or at least choose to, present a certain façade to the world. They take their place in the yellow pages of the phone book, or the church advertisements page of the Sunday newspaper. There they find it important to look important, staid, authoritative, respectable and thus dull. Dull, dull, dull. Young people especially see only the church of church bulletins and tickets to church suppers; of people who leave their interestingness at the door when they enter the sanctuary; of sinners who fake boring saintliness and saints who don't let their sinnerhood show; of suppressed emotions and obscured or petty conflict; of ritualized and routinized joy and patterned and prescriptive—ugh!—"caring and sharing."

On college campuses I meet survivors and rejecters of such boredom. During their childhood and high-school years many of them came to admire ministers who reached out to them. But they dismiss as ennui factories the old "First Church" back home. Often I want to reach out to them, too, and all but scream: "You don't know what you're missing! If you want high drama in the midst of apparently ordinary lives, turn invisible and make the rounds with your minister!"

Here we get to make the rounds with one busy but reflective minister who is at his best when he speaks out of congregational experience. Try this experiment: chapter by chapter, compare Barnes when he's doing what we teach people to do at theological schools to Barnes the pastor. On the former occasions he cites, adduces end-note material, replicates material from elsewhere. Well and good; he has a fine ear for hearing and an excellent voice for passing things on. And good taste, I would say, having spotted myself in the notes. But anyone can do such drawing upon others. You will find yourself most moved and informed by what Barnes thinks about what happens when he is in sick rooms or at grave side, confronting a congregation or trying to make his family fit into his rounds. You will find some shockers along the way, including a reference in chapter one to a personal and family circumstance that colors other chapters as it shadows his whole life.

One of my theories about ministers in congregations is this: They have to do some sort of moonlighting in order to live toward their potential and be interesting to others. Those whose whole life and energy go into meeting the demands of "the people who hire them," the congregations who do have a right to make first call upon them, tend to be consumed. In their genuine effort to be available to people, they find themselves being too available in matters where they have no expertise. He ends up serving as chauffeur for the Boy Scouts, though he may be the worst driver in the congregation. Though her skills in administration may be weak, she may become the head administrator of all subdepartments of her church.

Moonlighting, by which I mean having some source or demand for energies beyond the congregation, benefits the believers who make up the gathered group. The minister's whole context for the development of identity, ego and satisfaction is not then confined to a closed group of people. In being their servant, she does not become their slave. If someday a particular program does not work for the congregation, an experience in the Zone of Moonlight may prove applicable. Or, if he is tempted to pride in the parish, getting knocked around "out there"— on the zoning board or the hospital board, in a classroom as student or teacher, or in a club or caucus—will be salutary.

What Barnes does not tell readers is that, while having a ministry busy enough to consume him, in Colorado Springs and Chicago and now Madison, he has also pursued master's and doctoral degrees. I have worked with him through the decision to undertake the work and as he has proceeded through classes, seminars, examinations and now dissertation writing. The program he followed is demanding for full-time students who are on the scene. It is especially arduous for someone who must travel three hours for appointments with advisers and visits to the research library. Picture him driving along, flipping through piles of cards representing vocabularies of foreign languages he must learn, or listening to taped lectures. The interplay of a life of devotion to the parish and the vocation of scholarship informs his ministry and this book.

What I find most attractive and useful about this book is not the fact that it comes from a pastor who succeeds in showing how exciting the pastorate can be. I am taken with its thesis, the heart and soul of the book. Barnes has read and listened enough to know that what we call "the hunger for wholeness" is all too often met with the false promise that it can be fully satisfied on earth. He has the honesty to point out that this or that regimen or discipline, this or that therapy or philosophy, or even this or that way of being Christian cannot bring everything to a coherent, integrated, realized whole.

Why not? It is not in the biblical promises. Fulfillment has never yet come. It is dishonest to advertise that one has it to offer. It's frustrating to respond to such promises and then to find success denied.

But if this were a book that only described limits, it would be unsatisfying. To learn about limits and failure, all one has to do is look out the window or at the newspaper or television or into the heart. What one does with a life that falls short of realized wholeness: that is the present point and the plot. I am so eager to have you be drawn into the plot and to begin to get the author's point that I shall not detail any part of them. Read on.

Martin E. Marty
The University of Chicago

———

THE LORD GOD TOOK THE MAN AND PUT HIM IN THE

GARDEN OF EDEN TO WORK IT AND TAKE CARE

OF IT. AND THE LORD GOD COMMANDED THE

MAN, "YOU ARE FREE TO EAT FROM ANY TREE IN THE

GARDEN; BUT YOU MUST NOT EAT FROM THE TREE OF THE

KNOWLEDGE OF GOOD AND EVIL, FOR WHEN

YOU EAT OF IT YOU WILL SURELY DIE."

GENESIS 2:15-17

TELLING
THE
TRUTH

1

The organ swells as the choir begins to sing. I stand at the Communion table alongside the other pastor and the elders of the church. Down the aisle in front of us, the Christmas Eve worshipers wait in procession to receive the body of Christ and the cup of salvation. As each comes forward to the table, there is a split second in which my eye catches his or hers. In this privileged glance between pastor and parishioner is contained all the shared memories of the year's hard truth. One after another, we remember the marriage that was lost, the child that died, the cherished old lover whose brain has been tortured by Alzheimer's. I say only, "The body of Christ." It is all that can be said. It is all the gospel says. It is enough.

On this night we are celebrating the birth of our hope. It is one of the greatest experiences of the church. Christ has come. Everything is different, but the truth of the matter is that little has changed. Year after year, Christmas sermons will proclaim that because Christ has come the human situation has been fundamentally altered—all things have become new. But on both sides of the pulpit there is the nagging doubt that in spite of that hope not much will really change next year.

These are my people. Over the years, in times of joy and in times of heartache, I have been invited into the realities of their lives. I know the burdens they carry as they make their way to that Communion table. I am overwhelmed at the courage it takes for many of them to find their place in that procession. That some continue to hope at all is as much of a miracle as I will ever need to see. As I watch them walk back to their pews, I ask myself, "Why do they keep coming here? What have they found in this broken Christ?"

The Myth of Wholeness
Hope arises out of the hard truth of how things are. Christians will always live carrying in one hand the promises of how it will be and in the other the hard reality of how it is. To deny either is to hold only half the truth of the gospel.

But our dual burden drives us a little crazy. We long for simplistic reassurances. We want to know that we have found a gospel that will vanquish the hard realities. To live with a promise and its contradictions is the most heroic challenge of the Christian faith.

In recent years, particularly in the West, we have drifted into a belief that we can live without this tension. We now assure ourselves that God wants us to live without the needs and realistic limitations that we admit so reluctantly. Christians, in particular, believe that they should have found the secret to living whole and fulfilling lives.

Much of the spiritual advice Christians offer to each other assumes that wholeness is God's great desire for humanity. This assumption betrays a tendency to psychologize the doctrine of redemption. Salvation thus becomes a matter of healing the hurts suffered earlier in life, and need is perceived as a flaw in the original work of God—who must have made us to be whole creatures.

Wholeness is in style. But even though the term is used constantly, it is rarely defined. Typically, Christians who talk about wholeness mean that all of the individual must come under the healing work of God. The wholistic teachers want to avoid a spirituality that has no implications for the real needs of life. They are certainly to be commended for asserting that the gospel has meaning for the nitty-gritty of life. But the meaning they think it has is another matter. They are sure the gospel promises that God is working to restore us to a created condition of being complete. About that some of us have doubts. Serious doubts.

Few people claim to actually be whole, but many have committed their lives to attaining wholeness. Between their spiritual disciplines, their current psychotherapy and their commitment to heal the hurts of the past, they hope at least to move in the direction of wholeness.

The yearning for wholeness is intense today because many feel so fractured and torn. They are torn by the competing demands of work and home, of spouse and child, and of the church that keeps asking for more of their time and energy. They are torn by dreams for the future that are ridiculed by failures of the past. They are torn by the longing to get life right and the nagging suspicion that they are fatally flawed, and they are torn absolutely apart by the craving to be loved and the terrified fear of being known. If only they were whole, if only they could fix all the parts of life that don't seem to work, then they would be okay.

So out of compassion, someone tells them all of it can be changed, because—and this is the seductive part—God wants to meet their needs. Out of compassion, someone unintentionally lies. The call to wholeness is being issued in the sermons, journals, workshops, and advice industry of both conservative and liberal quarters of the church. But we don't find it in Scripture.

What we find in Scripture is the incredible promise that God has broken into our brokenness to find us there. There is no promise that, having found us, he will paste our fractured lives back together.

This doesn't mean that all of life doesn't have to be brought under the healing of God. It does. But God's healing doesn't fit exactly with our yearnings to have the pain taken away. As a church member with cancer once told me, "There is a big difference between healing and avoiding death." God's healing has more to do with learning to worship than it does with getting life fixed. What God is eager to heal is the sickness of the soul and the blindness of the heart that take us down a painful road away from his love. Worship is the means by which our eyes are opened.

In worshiping God we realize we were never created to be whole. God will not restore what we were never intended to have. What we were created to enjoy is fellowship with God, who alone is whole and complete.

Nowhere in the Bible are we told that God wants to give us wholeness. What God wants to give us is himself. If we really believed that, it would be enough. In fact, it would be more than enough. It would overwhelm us.

The effect of our fascination with wholeness is that it embarks us on a journey for which there is no end, a journey that takes us further away from God. He invites us to journey in a different direction.

Impossible Dreams
In his book *The Sacred and the Profane,* Mircea Eliade, the late his-

torian of religions, described the religious life of a nomadic tribe of Australians, the Achilpa. According to their creation story, after the god Numbakula had made the heavens and the earth, he cut down a gum tree, anointed it with blood, and placed it between the heavens and the earth. He then climbed the pole and disappeared into the sky. Following the legend, the Achilpa made their own gum-tree pole. As the tribe wandered from place to place, they chose their direction according to the bend at the end of the pole. No matter where they went, as long as the pole was in their midst, their little world had order, meaning, and security.

One day, however, there was a tragic accident: the sacred pole broke. Looking aghast at their broken pole, the entire tribe was thrown into despair. They wandered aimlessly for a while, but soon they lay down on the ground and waited for the sky to come crashing down.[1]

We all have some Achilpa pole that we use to make sense of our world. It gives us direction, security, and it holds off anomie—that fearful state of meaninglessness.[2] No matter where life takes us, as long as the pole is in place, we can rest assured that our world will not fall apart.

In our contemporary culture, we have developed such religious devotion to the totems of fulfillment and wholeness that we think we cannot survive without them. It isn't that getting the larger home with the two-car garage or the new intimate relationship will keep our life together. That isn't really what gives us meaning. It is in *craving* these things that we find life's meaning. As soon as we get what we have been chasing, we will find ourselves yearning for something else.

So it doesn't really matter what we say we are craving—a body that won't make us ashamed, a more significant job, the birth of a child, or even the courage to tell our parents how angry we are at what they did to us. As long as we keep craving and yearning for something, life will hold together, because we are on the way to finding what we want.

This craving to fill life's empty places forms the cosmic axis around which our world turns. No matter where the search leads us—through one relationship after another, through job after job, into therapy, recreation, and achievements, and even through different churches—we continue to believe this next thing will fulfill us. That is our sacred hope.

In the pastorate, I have many opportunities to hear the words "if only. . . ." It is one of the few expressions that does not seem to have generational boundaries. Typically, it is first heard from squirming young teenagers who can't wait to get away from home. "If only I can get to college, then I will be free to make my own decisions and be who I want to be." The collegiate's line is, "If only I can make it out of college and land that dream job, then I am going to have the money and the time to start living." Frequently, however, those first dream jobs turn into nightmares. Then the lament is changed to "If only I could find a better job."

Often at the young adult stage of life, romantic relationships become serious commitments. Those who aren't married frequently wish they were. Those who realize that neither their job nor their marriage will be totally fulfilling start to say, "If only we had a child." In time even parents who have willingly made great sacrifices for their children find themselves thinking, "If only we can get the kids through college, then our freedom, and our money, will be all ours once again." The children don't have to be gone too long, though, before these same parents start to say, "If only we could get the kids to visit a little more often, it sure would be nice." When the health problems that inevitably accompany aging start to appear, they are sure they'd be content if only they had their health back.

We can cry "if only" all the way through life, until at some point, possibly in a nursing home, we are lamenting, "If only I had lived differently." It is a sad way to go through life. No one plans on wishing one's life away. It happens frequently, though, because like the nomadic Achilpa we wander into the future with our hope that in the next place our world will come together.

Rather than returning to their own life-giving creation story, Christians tend to live by the myths of the world. In fact, we pray for direction from our God and hope he will lead us into the place where we just know we will be okay, if only we can find it. Many pray to reassure themselves that God is invested in the dreams that have been battered by the harshness of life. But those dreams may be born out of a myth that is not ours.

Our creation story does not call us to roam through life in the pursuit of happiness. In fact, that is the very thing from which we are saved. Our story portrays the great journey of God into his limited and needy creation.

Biblical hope is found when Christians hear the gospel and take their place in the great processions of the body of Christ. The proclamation of that hope is that in communing with Christ we discover all the grace we need to live joyful but limited lives. For in communing with God we encounter the mystery of his presence with us. Joy is something we *receive,* and we receive it only through the strange activity of God.

The beginning place for this spirituality usually is the shattering of our earlier hopes for getting life together. We have feared that when we lose our dreams the sky will surely fall down upon us. We are most ready for grace when we confess that fear. In the words of Jürgen Moltmann, "In the forsakenness of the cross of Jesus Christ, God has taken on the godforsakenness of us all."[3] In the moment in which we feel abandoned by both our dreams and the God we thought would save them for us—in precisely that moment we are ready to receive God's true salvation. It is then we discover that God wants to save us, not our dreams.

The Christian Subculture

A vast amount of energy goes into maintaining the hope that if only we will live as Christians, life can be as we have dreamed. The world around us, so plentiful in illustrations of how hard life can be, has become something Christians have to flee. We must flee the world if we are to maintain the myth that in finding Christ we have found the key to wholeness.

Many Christians live in a subculture in which the ideal of being the new creation has become the norm. Yet given the gap between the ideal and the real, the norms of their religious culture are pretend norms.

They pretend that by circling the wagons of the church they can hold off the harshness of the secular world around them. They have their own fellowship groups, jargon, hero figures, music (both sacred and rock) and even political lobbyists. It adds up to an isolated religious culture created to protect them, and their children, from the arrows of secular influence.

The effect is to put the church in competition with the world rather than in loving mission to it. We chastise the world for its commitment to the formulas of success and materialism, but we advertise our own products, our Bible studies and devotional methods, as the best way to reach the mythical land of happiness. This is the presupposition of many of our books and videos on marriage, family life, relationships and even money management. The advice peddlers assure us that Christian principles will offer greater success in these areas of struggle. Yet the truth is that our formulas don't work a whole lot better than those of the world. That is what makes the subculture—and its isolation from reality—necessary.

There is no greater threat to the religious subculture than the humanity of Christian leaders. Our modern-day holy men are supposed to live more deeply within the Christian truth than others who do not have the same training, experience, or ordination from God. When church leaders betray the marks of human character, or worse yet, succumb to temptation, their failure undermines our ability to believe and sell the myth that Christians have found the secret to fulfillment.

The real difficulty we have with these leaders is not that they sinned, but that they have betrayed our dream. When the same sins are committed by those who are new to the faith, they are frequently shrugged off as the mistakes of those who have yet to learn the disciplines of spiritual living. That story never makes the newspapers. But when the popular teacher of spiritual disciplines illustrates to the whole world that his spirituality has not alleviated the deep need for something more, then we consider it fraud.

In recent years some sectors of the Protestant world have been rocked by the fall of their role models. It was bound to happen. It has happened before, and it will certainly happen again—as long as we continue to nurture the hope that somewhere, somebody has found the way to get God in our pockets.

The biblical truth is that the church was never meant to live as a subculture, and our witness is not to a religious formula for fulfillment and happiness. The opening chapters of Genesis clearly teach that we have been created to live in gardens in which we do not have it all. Ironically, we take refuge from the world in the Christian subculture in an effort to achieve the world's aspirations of wholeness and fulfillment. But in seeking spiritual formulas to fulfill our dreams, we become more worldly than ever.

When God's Promises Don't Work Out
One of my seminary teachers once cautioned that any theology that does not hold up in the emergency rooms of life must be held suspect. It is in those places of crisis and loss that our Christian beliefs come

under their greatest test. A wife bids tearful good-by to her young husband who is dying, Christian parents struggle with their child's drug addiction, a wife finds a note from her husband on the refrigerator, announcing that he has left and won't be back. Sooner or later someone asks, "Oh my God, why?"

When Christians find themselves in these crises they frequently feel betrayed. They have faithfully maintained the disciplines of their faith and have committed themselves wholeheartedly to church, Bible studies, and mission projects. But none of that has protected them from crisis.

Even if Christians have somehow avoided times of deep crisis, they cannot escape a plaguing sense of dissatisfaction with some part of their life. Perhaps the job is boring, or the relationship with parents has become only more frustrating with time, or there is a marriage that may not degenerate into divorce but is certainly never going to have the level of intimacy one dreams about. We expect these uncomfortable situations in the lives of those who are not Christians, but we believe Christians should be able to live differently.

It is true that the Bible offers us a different understanding of life from that of the world around us, but it is not true that biblical living will protect us from either crisis or unfulfillment. In fact, there are times when real life seems to mock the promises of Scripture.

Not long ago an old farmer was buried. He was a Christian and in fact would be described by some as a pillar of his small country church. The old man appeared to have lived a good long life. At the graveside, his wife and children said their good-bys, the minister commended the old man's body to the ground and his soul to the arms of God, and it all seemed to have had a storybook ending.

But those who knew the truth knew something was missing—the prodigal son who still had not come home. The old man had taken to his grave a scriptural promise, "Train up a child in the way he should go, and when he is old he will not depart from it." No one really knew what had gone wrong, but the old man's son, once a model of Christian leadership, was lost.

No one knew where the son was or what he was doing. The only thing anyone knew for sure was that his name had been about the only word that could make the old farmer start to cry. For years the aging father had rehearsed all the experiences he had shared with the boy, all the boy's early signs of promise, all the expectations they had built together. Year after year he had told himself that soon his son would return. But the boy had stayed away, isolated in his anger, refusing to be reconciled. The rest of the family learned to avoid talking about the son, but the old man had persisted in hoping that someday he would return. After all, he would say, "Train up a child in the way he should go. . . ." He had never been able to finish that sentence.

As the father grew older and more feeble, the other family members had thought the son would surely come home. Time was running out on the father's faith. But the son never came.

Even at the funeral, they just knew that somehow he would get there. As they gathered beside the grave, each of the brothers and sisters stole glances around the cemetery, hoping the son would appear to make his peace over the father's grave. The mother quietly cried. But the old man's boy—who is my father—never showed up.

To this day, the child that was raised in the way he should go remains lost. My father was lost to my grandfather, who grieved for his son till he day he died. And he is lost to me. There are very few days that I don't think about him. I suppose I have inherited Grandfather's lament. "Train up a child in the way he should go, and when he is old he will not depart from it." But he did.

Why does that happen? Why do we spend our days banking on promises that are never fulfilled? Perhaps it happens because the promises are not confined to our expectations. God has never made himself accountable to his creatures, and his promises often appear to leave us forsaken.

As a people of faith, we are right to build our lives around those promises. That is what God's people have done since the days of Abraham. That is what the church does every Sunday when it prays, "Thy kingdom come."

In relying on God's promises we testify to the world that we believe in the God who is committed to his creation, and in the face of all our deathlike experiences we will continue to believe that. That is what living by faith means. Yet as Job learned from the voice out of the whirlwind, we will never understand the ways of God. We will not understand the strange timing of the promises he makes. In the forsakenness of Christ on the cross, it certainly seemed as if God had missed again. God did not spare his Son this bitterly hard part of the journey. If we call ourselves followers of Christ, we cannot expect God to save us from it, either.

Religious Sentimentality

One of the great dangers to the church's credibility these days is our sentimentality. It is seen in our fascination with telling story after story that all follow the same tired plot. Someone had been dealt a bad hand. Perhaps it is a physical handicap, or an emotional handicap that resulted from the loss of a loved one, or a dream that has been shattered by reality. Some variances on the story line even include mistakes we made in our life before we met God. Inevitably, however, these sentimental plots all turn into good news at the moment the Christian meets God. With the power of God on our side, the handicaps of life become mere hurdles over which we spring. In the end we are made whole, and, more important, God is off the hook, for once again "all things worked together for good."

We don't hear many sermon illustrations about old fathers dying of broken hearts. Our inspirational magazines don't carry stories about the despair of events like the massacre at Tiananmen Square. We don't like to spend too much of our worship time on activities as depressing as Communion. We would rather put Psalm 100 to music than Psalm 22. All of this is because we think the good news of the gospel has to have a happy ending—now.

As the comedian Bob Newhart is fond of saying, "I would like to make a motion that we face reality." Not all the stories in Scripture have happy endings. Not all the heroes of faith saw the fulfillment of the promises they had chased their whole lives. The only land we are certain Abraham owned at the end of his life was the burial plot he purchased for Sarah. Moses only got close enough to the promised land to see it from the mountain where he died. David's life certainly didn't end on a high note. Jeremiah will always be remembered as the weeping prophet. Jesus, himself, wears the identity of Isaiah's suffering servant—a man of sorrows who was acquainted with grief. The apostles all were committed to the promises of what would become of the new church, but at their deaths the stability and future of the church were far from secure. God's history is not confined to our span of life, and his promises are not delivered just in the nick of time for us. The church's witness in the world will go much further if we tell the truth, even when that means struggling with its implications. The psalms are unflinchingly honest in expressing such struggles.

My God, my God, why have you forsaken me?
Why are you so far from saving me,
so far from the words of my groaning?
O my God, I cry out by day, but you do not answer,

27

by night, and am not silent.

Yet you are enthroned as the Holy One;

    you are the praise of Israel. (Ps 22:1-3)

The great witness of this lament is that David continued to believe in the enthroned holiness of God though he personally suffered from God's absence. There is no shortage of opportunities for Christians to lament the absence of God in our violent, hungry, and disease-ridden world. These are opportunities for faith to have real meaning. It does not take faith to live by miraculous signs of God's involvement. Faith is the substance of things we hope for when there is no sign that God will pull through.

Demanding Grace

What distinguishes Christians from the world is not that we have figured out how to live more successfully, more fully, or even more securely than the non-Christian. None of that is promised to the first disciples who followed Christ, and it certainly is not promised to us either. Many scriptural promises refer to the "good work" that God is doing in our lives, but as Paul reminds us, those promises are not brought to completion till the day of Jesus Christ (Phil 1:6). The promise God fulfills now is that in our discipleship we will find new meaning and vision for our lives. That meaning comes not from gaining life, but from losing it as we follow the Christ who calls us to live by grace.

Grace can be demanding. As a pastor, I am struck by how seldom we recognize grace when it shows up. That is usually because it rides into our lives upon a vehicle that will take us to places we'd rather not go. We are sure it will lead us to our death. Turns out it is the way to salvation.

By definition, grace is a gift. As Dietrich Bonhoeffer reminds us, however, it is not a cheap gift. Once it has hold of our life it is relentless in its demand that everything be changed.

It was the call of God's grace that led Abraham and Sarah away from their home toward the promise of a new land. It was grace that invited the disciples to drop their nets and follow Jesus, and it was grace that knocked Paul off the course of his effort to become a great Pharisee. Certainly no one in Scripture earned grace. It seems that nobody even asked for it. It did save their lives, but that salvation never looked like what they'd had in mind.

The grace that many of us would prefer is the one that isn't demanding, but instead supports our agendas for fulfillment. God's grace, however, almost always comes as a disruption of those agendas. Grace strips away all our busy plans to save ourselves and calls us to the new road of God's salvation. Not only does that road not promise to lead us to wholeness, it is often even harder than the road on which we started life. Jesus was brutally honest in predicting that he would fragment and divide us from our families and former places of identity. What makes the Christian journey worthwhile is only that we are following Jesus.

It's likely that at the end of their lives Abraham, Sarah, the disciples, and Paul all would have agreed that receiving God's grace was the best thing that could have happened to them. There are plenty of indications, though, that along the way they had their doubts. Since most of life is lived along the way, we spend most of our time wondering what is so gracious about the grace we have received. It is a good question because it tells the truth, and telling the truth always leads us back to Jesus.

The call of Christ to pick up our cross and follow him is the most gracious offer a person can receive, but it is not an invitation to the good life. Rather, it is an invitation to the life we were created to have—a life that bears the marks of what is missing in the middle of our garden.

A New Look at Genesis

The first three chapters of Genesis contain critically important insights about our created situation. These texts have too often served as a battleground for theological and scientific conflicts over the authority of Scripture. Frequently they have been hauled into court to stand against "humanistic" textbooks in public debates over what we will teach our children. Sadly, in arguing over the exact nature of the historicity of the Genesis account, Christians have often ignored the power of its message for life today.

Seldom do we refer to the creation narratives in the debates over current ethical questions or the debates about debt, materialism, and broken homes. Yet on such issues these texts can be of considerable help. Genesis 1—3 proclaims to the consuming world around us that we were never meant to have it all. Neither the persistent cravings of the individual nor the more dangerous collective appetites of societies are ever going to be filled. That's the good news. It serves as a daily reminder that we are not gods, but a people in need of grace.

The great symbol of this created limitation is the forbidden tree that was planted in the middle of the garden. Right in the center of the good garden was a daily reminder that Adam and Eve did not have it all. Every day Adam and Eve had to walk by that piece of the garden that was out of bounds. Had the tree been off in some forgotten corner of the garden, it would have been much easier to ignore. But Scripture makes it clear that the tree was in the *middle* of the garden—it could not be disregarded.

The absence of the fruit was even part of what defined Adam and Eve as creatures. As long as they lived with the daily experience of need, there was little opportunity to think of themselves as gods. The temptation of the serpent was to remind them of that very fact. The absence in the midst of our lives continues to be our greatest vulnerability, and the reach for forbidden fruit eternally symbolizes our reach for something more than mere creatures can ever have.

Be careful about what this does and does not mean. It does not mean that all neediness is inherently good and therefore we should avoid feeding the hungry and binding up the wounds of those who need healing. It doesn't mean that we should reject the marvelous gifts of medicine, technology, and therapeutic psychology. It certainly doesn't mean that Christians are excused from taking responsibility for the great needs of people around us. But it does mean that we must go about the mission of the church without assuming that our goal is to fix everything.

To live with absence in the midst of our gardens means that the deep yearnings of the spirit are part of what makes us human. Most important, our need always provides the opportunity to renew our dependency on the grace of God. What we call need or a "defect" can become our greatest altar for true worship.

For us to live fully can only mean to embrace both the heights and the depths, the joy and the pain of real life. All of it has a place in our garden. All of it makes us who are—part of the good creation of God.

WHEN THE LORD GOD MADE THE EARTH AND THE

HEAVENS . . . THERE WAS NO MAN TO WORK THE GROUND.

. . . THE LORD GOD FORMED THE MAN FROM

THE DUST OF THE GROUND AND BREATHED INTO HIS

NOSTRILS THE BREATH OF LIFE, AND THE MAN

BECAME A LIVING BEING.

GENESIS 2:4-7

REMAKING
OR
RECEIVING

2

In our city, many of the clergy occasionally get together to wrestle with major ethical issues. Sometimes we discuss these issues with community leaders, the media, or even our congressional representatives. The topics include all the hot debates of the day—abortion, euthanasia, rationing of health care, racism, homosexuality, public education. Almost everyone has opinions on these issues, and they usually defend their positions with passion and intelligence.

But I have discovered that what the clergy does best is to inject humility into these debates. Since we belong to communities of faith, each of us can find someone in our parish whose life has been torn apart by just about any of these issues. For us they are never just "issues." They have names, and faces, and stories that would break your heart. And it is the broken heart that is frequently missing from the public debates. If churches told their stories more often it might help us find our way through the issues. It would also help us find our way back to God. Brokenness leads to humility, and humility always opens our lives to the Creator.

Questions We Cannot Answer

I had been ordained for only two months when the call came that one of our parishioners was dying. By the time I got to the hospital, Mrs. Miller was already meeting with her husband's doctors. They were asking her to decide how much longer they should artificially sustain his life. There was little hope that he would ever breathe without the respirator.

Actually, we had thought he was dying the week before, when he had gone into cardiac arrest after an extended illness. He had been revived only after a "full code" was followed, which meant the doctors opened his chest and massaged his heart. By then he had lost too much oxygen, though, and the doctors were certain he had suffered brain damage. Through the agonizing days of the following week we had prayed and cried and hoped he would beat the odds. Now it appeared that the miracle was not going to come. Mr. Miller had little hope of recovering.

Trying to remain honest about the limitations of their science, the doctors insisted on saying "little hope" rather than no hope. That was the part that bothered Mrs. Miller the most. *Little* hope. If his chances were one in ninety-nine, shouldn't she keep him on the respirator? What if he beat the odds? The doctors patiently explained the grim prospects of an extended coma that could last months, even years, with the assistance of the life-sustaining machines. The tired and frightened woman was out of energy, money, and the ability to make hard decisions.

This was not the ending she had envisioned for this man she had loved over fifty years. It didn't fit with the deaths portrayed in movies and novels. There was nothing romantic about this death. No intimate good-bys on a quilt-covered bed at home. No last kiss. Just the whir of the respirator and an unbelievably painful decision. Should she sign the papers that would result in turning little hope into no hope? The tears streamed down her face, and she looked at me and asked, "What should I do?"

As I drove home from the hospital that day, I thought about how proud I had been two months before at my graduation from seminary. I had been trained to help people with the good news of God's love for them in Jesus Christ. I had worked through the writings of the best theological scholars and church historians. But in that doctor's office there had been nothing in my bag of theological tools to help me with the simple question that has haunted me ever since—"What should I do?"

In that moment my pride had been transformed into deep humility. I didn't know the answer. I had done well in seminary and had always known the answers there, but I was incapable of certainty as a practicing pastor. In part, that is because real life is not as clear as it is in textbooks. On a broader level, however, our difficulty with such questions is the result of our society's refusal to recognize limitations. Fifty years ago, when Mr. and Mrs. Miller were married, no one had dreamed that some-day one of them would have to decide whether or not to keep the other one alive. Technological sophistication, we are discovering, leads to terrifying questions without answers—such as, "When is life over?" Pastors are not the only ones who are uncertain about that. This issue is plaguing the medical and legal professions today. Pastors, however, sit beside the families who are tormented by having to answer the question. So for them, this is never just an "issue."

Day after day, Mrs. Miller would go to the hospital, stroke her husband's hair and ask him, "What should I do?" We wrestled with her choice for three agonizing weeks before she was ready to make the decision she hated herself for making. I will never forget sitting with her in the waiting room with our hands clenched tightly together, knowing the doctors were disconnecting the machines in his room. We cried. We reassured ourselves. And we prayed. Mostly, we prayed for deliverance.

The question of when life is over is a real-life dilemma that is breaking somebody's heart every day, and I feel certain it is a dilemma for which we will never have clear answers. Maybe humans were never designed to carry the great weight of such decisions. It is more than enough. It is too much.

How, then, do we live with progress? Certainly not all of our technological developments are inherently wrong. Nothing in Scripture categorically opposes our efforts to improve social conditions or physical well-being. In fact, Scripture encourages the right use of the world around us. The question isn't whether we should progress as a people. The question is how we avoid progressing into the disasters that always follow humanity's attempts to play God.

A Second Look at Stewardship

I believe there is a clear biblical rationale for progress and scientific research that will also help to keep us from crossing the boundaries of our limitations. That rationale is found in the biblical call to stewardship.

> Be fruitful and increase in number; fill the earth and subdue it. Rule over the fish of the sea and the birds of the air and over every living creature that moves on the ground. . . . God saw all that he had made, and it was very good. (Gen 1:28, 31)

The word "stewardship" is not a bit of religious jargon that we use to disguise our discussions about money. Rather, it refers to a biblical perspective on responsibility. All that we have, and all that is around us, has been entrusted to us to manage well. God has called humanity to "subdue" the good creation that surrounds us in order to take care of it. That means, in effect, that we should learn all we can from the laws of nature. But it also means that this knowledge must always further our ability to care for God's created order. Would all of our technological improvements and all of our scientific research meet this criterion? Often our efforts to improve life are actually attempts to alter creation because we don't think it is good enough. Altering the created order goes beyond the job description of good stewards. We serve as good stewards of life when we develop medicines to fight disease. We violate that role when medical research assumes it can prevent death by mechanically maintaining the breath of life for months and years. When has that ever yielded more real life? It certainly didn't further the life of Mr. Miller. If anything, the denial of his death actually became a denial of his life.

As stewards we serve God and his creation; as sinners we become gods who attempt to change creation's order.

Stewardship defines both the opportunities and the limitations of life. We have a wonderful opportunity both to develop and to enjoy the life we've received. Good stewards will invest heavily in their own lives, relationships, and work. As members of a larger community, stewards should readily commit themselves to social aspirations—better programs and strategies of providing care to others and promoting peace and justice. But foundational to good stewardship is an awareness of who it is that owns the garden we live in. What stewards *cannot* do is pretend that the garden is theirs to re-create. Whenever we call God's good creation "not good enough," we are making that pretense.

Forbidden Words

The Bible makes a careful (and very important) distinction between the

Creator and the creatures. It is the Creator alone who utters the sacred and powerful words "Let there be." In the Hebrew text, the term that is used for those words is *bara*. That word is never used in Scripture to refer to the creativity of humans. It is the unique activity of God—the work of bringing life and order into existence.[1]

This distinctive activity of God is fundamental to the theology of the Old Testament authors. For them, history and creation were inseparable. God's creative work served as the stage on which his saving work began and continued. The *bara* of God was seen not only in the creation of life and order but also in his subsequent redemptive acts in history. The creation of a covenant, a people, a nation, and a future, are all attributed to the *bara* of God. It is by the divine initiative and Word that all of these came about—not by the work of his creatures.

The New Testament maintains the same distinction. It is in Christ, the Word of God, that the Christian has become a new creation (2 Cor 5:17). The same Spirit of God that once moved over the face of the waters, bringing light and order to the darkness and chaos (Gen 1:2), moves over the life of the Christian to bring God's good work to completion in the day of Jesus Christ (Phil 1:6). We are not able to create "rightness" in our lives; it is only by grace that we receive that work from God (Eph 2:8-9).

Throughout Scripture, the people of God are constantly reminded of this Creator-creature distinction, and they find identity in it. Their relationship to God always exists as that of the sustaining Creator to creatures who would perish without him. In the Old Testament, it is the task of prophets like Isaiah and Jeremiah to remind the oppressed and captive Hebrews that their Creator is sovereign over the course of history and will redeem his people through his creative power and wisdom. We can appreciate the New Testament's central themes of grace and salvation only by identifying with the Old Testament's story of the creatures' determination to wander away from their Creator.

Making the Creator into a Creature

In creating humanity from the dust of the earth, God created something with which he must never be confused. He forever remains the One who is holy and sacred in our midst. This means that Christians must always hold together two beliefs about God. On the one hand, we cherish a very relational understanding of the God who gave us his Son out of love. God has revealed himself as the Good Shepherd who seeks each lost lamb, who heals the brokenhearted, and who graciously restores us to new life. Yet our Scriptures also portray a sacred Creator who can never be a god of our own making. This dimension of God should frighten us a bit, reminding us that God is not predictable. He is never just the God for *us;* and while he is a God of grace, he is also a God of judgment who stands against our self-asserted claims to power and wisdom.

True worship, then, must draw us irresistibly to our Shepherd of compassion and bid us to bow down once we've found ourselves at his feet. Without the caring side of God we have no reason for hope. But without an appreciation of the sacred mystery of God, our relational emphasis too easily becomes petty and self-serving.

By definition, the words "holy" and "sacred" refer to that which is beyond our manageability. God cannot be contained by our expectations of his character or our dreams of what he will do for us. Of course, this reality is disturbing. The forbidden tree planted in the middle of everyone's garden is a reminder that God has not revealed all of his work or plans to us. And that can drive us wild with insecurity.

There is more to God than we know—more than we will ever know. Unable to live with a God we cannot fully understand, and thus can never control, we rush to find alternative gods who promise to be more manageable. Ultimately, however, we discover that these alternative gods of success, relationships, or cherished possessions are no more manageable than the Creator God. In fact, we soon discover that they have actually enslaved us with the teasing hope that we'll finally find fulfillment if only we bow to them one more time.

Recently a successful businessman in our church invited me to lunch. For a long time he discussed the frustrations of maintaining his success. Then he sighed deeply, looked at me, and quietly said, "You know, I am so tired of having to make more and more money. Success is a relentless game, and I can never be sure if I am winning or losing."

The predicament of many is just that simple and just that complicated. Money is not a very satisfying god to worship. Most of us would readily agree with that statement. But we are still sorely tempted to bow to this god, and once we do, money proves a hard taskmaster. It does not liberate us. From early childhood we have learned how to consume more and more, but very few parents teach their children how to let go of the need for money.

Typically, by the time we realize that we are trapped it is too late. There is precious little time left for the things that matter in life. It is after the kids are away at college that parents realize how little time was spent playing with them. It is as a father takes his "little girl" down the aisle on her wedding day that he wonders where the time went. He has spent so much of his time being a good provider that he has forever lost the opportunity to give himself to the daughter he loves. A young couple knock themselves out to buy a nicer home than they can really afford, only to discover that their souls now belong to the house, and they will have to make huge sacrifices just to keep their mortgage. These scenarios occur all too often. They are the common signs of idolatry.

Those who bow before the idols of hard work and success hope their devout commitment will provide security and fulfillment. But the gods mortals create have always left them drained and spent. The Hebrews were so intimidated by their unpredictable God that they cried out to have gods "of wood and stone" like those of neighboring peoples. The gods fashioned by the hands of creatures stand as monuments to what hard work can accomplish, but in truth they suck away human life. As my parishioner said, such gods are relentlessly demanding.

Making the Creature into a Creator

The distinction between the Creator and the creature is blurred when we see humanity as something other than mere creatures. The emotional weight of living as a simple creature among creatures is too great for most people to bear. We tell ourselves that such a precarious existence belongs to animals and plant life, not to us. It threatens us to the core of our being to think that we are subject to the same laws of nature as the dead dog on the side of the road. Surely, if we just work hard we can be something more—and in being something more we'll gain significance, security, and a better life. We hear that promise all the time. "The world stands before you. Set your goals high, commit yourself to hard work, and you can be anything you want to be." Those were the last words spoken to my high-school graduating class. I will never forget them. As I walked across the stage to receive my diploma, the words kept ringing in my head, "Now I can be anything I want to be." For years I cherished that advice. I have probably even given it to other young graduates who appeared so full of life's possibilities. Eventually, though, I came to realize that the commencement speaker lied to us.

It is a beautiful lie. We love to hear it, and we hear it a lot. It certainly is not given only to young graduates. The lie is foundational to our advertising industry, our health and fitness programs, our employee-motivation speeches, and our well-meaning advice to friends. Sadly, it can even be found in the Christian church.

41

When a commercial tells us the lie, it holds up a product promising that this will help us be something other than what we are now. When Christians tell the lie, they assure us that God is rooting for us to become something great for the kingdom. But it could be that God hasn't asked everyone to make great contributions. Neither the products of the world nor the promises of the Christian life will ever make us into something other than what God has made us to be—creatures with limitations. We can't be anything we want to be. That is simply not how creatures are designed.

This truth is particularly difficult for members of the middle and upper classes of technologically sophisticated societies. Free from the threats of high infant mortality, starvation, violence, and anarchy, we have become smug in the security of our existence. For us, violence is news. To keep us current on the rest of the world, our magazines and televisions bring pictures of Third World conditions into our homes. As we gaze at the horrifying images of people in crisis, we wonder how those conditions could still exist.

Poverty continues because human beings are mere creatures. Like any living organism, when they are cut off from the basic necessities of life they will die. Sophisticated, secure humans have the audacity to forget that.

Whenever the insulated are forced to look at suffering, they long for the reassurance that it could never happen to them. The biblical depiction of human life as a journey from "dust to dust" doesn't seem to apply anymore. We marvel at great technological achievements and ask ourselves, "Dust? How could we just be dust? Look at what we have created!" Both individually and corporately, we have deceived ourselves into thinking that we can create our own worlds through a little knowledge and a lot of hard work. We appear secure and comfortable, and we are certainly well fed. Tragically, we use our technological capabilities not to provide for those who are in pain, but to protect ourselves from their hurts. Such an illusion is critical if we are going to believe the lie that we can be more than mere creatures.

For many years I have led church work camps in the barrios of Ciudad Juarez, Mexico, just across the border from El Paso, Texas. One of the fascinating dynamics of that experience is to study the contrasts in cultures that are separated only by a narrow river.

Once, after spending a week in one of the slum areas of Juarez, a few of us had to return to El Paso to pick up some hardware at a suburban shopping mall. The mall was like the shopping malls I have visited countless times in my own hometown. Only this time I was particularly struck by its absurdity.

Minutes before, we had left a whole society of people who were literally dying for good water. The most conservative estimates on infant mortality in Juarez are at 30 per cent. The primary cause of this tragedy is simply the diarrhea babies get from bacteria-laden water. These children are born and die in a hot, dusty, impoverished world.

In the American mall, clean water was used for decoration, endlessly spewing in colorful fountains. The mall was a pretend world of comfort. Like most indoor shopping malls, it was designed to make us feel as if we were outdoors, only not the real and often harsh outdoors. Trees lined the artificial cobblestone walkways, and large skylights filtered the sun's glaring light. We were coaxed to spend our money in beautiful, air-conditioned comfort. This pseudo-environment of our own making was preferable to the real one that oppressed families in the shacks five miles away. In fact, I could almost pretend the mall's world was the real one. The point is not that Christians should avoid shopping malls, although they do provide a frightening symbol of our need to create pretend worlds. The deeper issue is that we have to live as if the reality of the poor is part of our reality. The river that separates the slums of the world from its shopping malls is getting narrower all the time. Poverty is not just in the barrios of Mexico; it also exists in our own towns, and it seems to be getting more and more desperate wherever it is.

We cannot continue to create pretend worlds that allow us to live as if life were not a fragile thing. No one has the right to live unaffected by the sorrow of the world.

Embracing Life and Death

If we ever do forget our limitations, the fact of our mortality serves as a swift reminder. Death is a severe grace that protects us from the illusion of immortality. In my parish, it seems there is always someone dying. It also seems there is always someone who has just been born. Together these two events remind us that life can only be received. It is a precious gift that is ours only for a while.

Shortly after arriving as the new pastor of Christ Church, I met Don Murdoch. Don had been battling leukemia for many years, and no one really knew how much longer he would live. The process of dying had been a long and exhausting journey for Don and his family. It was my great honor to join them for the last year of that journey. During that time, I learned a great a deal about dying from Don. Dying is almost never beautiful. The only people who believe it is are those who have not watched it up close. When asked what he was learning through this experience, Don's favorite response was, "Don't get leukemia." Yet without being sentimental about a very unsentimental disease, he chose to embrace his death with the same vigor with which he had greeted the rest of his life.

Although I learned much from Don about "good death," I think he taught me even more about cherishing the brief gift of life. Watching his persistent fight to be alive, I was convicted that I have always taken my own life for granted. Watching his family grieve, I realized I had assumed my family would always be together, never knowing the pain of separation.

On the morning Don died with his wife, Ellen, holding his hand, I knew I had just seen a deep and vivid portrait of intimacy. I want to believe there will be someone to hold my hand when I die. For many of us, though, that seems too much to expect. So we deny our deaths and assure ourselves that we can get by on our own. We persevere in loneliness with heroic agendas, most of which allow no time for enjoying intimate moments of holding a lover's hand.

There is a striking contrast between Don's death and that of Mr. Miller, who slipped away under the anonymous mask of a respirator. Mr. Miller's final days were unfortunately death-denying; they distorted and contradicted his life, and almost destroyed the woman who loved him. Since Don had been allowed to embrace his limitations, he and Ellen could meet death as they had greeted the rest of their life together. He died as he had lived—with dignity and love.

After I left Ellen that morning and returned to the church office, there was a message waiting that another couple was at the hospital about to give birth to their third child. Theirs had been a difficult pregnancy, requiring the expectant mother to spend long months in bed. We had been anxious about the health of both mother and child.

By the time I arrived at the birthing room, the baby had been born, and his parents were holding him close. Everyone was fine. The parents looked up at me through tears of joy and relief, thrilled that they would be able to take home a strong and healthy child. New life had entered their family, and they would never be same. A new life had also entered our church, and because of him we would not be the same either.

What a day that was. The church is privileged to receive death and life within hours of each other. At these times it's as if a window opens briefly before us, inviting us to look beyond our lives to see the deep truth of creaturely existence: life is basically on loan to each of us. We receive it for a few years. We embrace it, love it, watch it grow and mature, and then at the end of our days we give it back to God. But our ability to let go of life when it is over is directly related to how well we received it while there was a hand to hold.

When we really believe that life is a gift, we enjoy it much more. If we really believed that life is too short to waste in playing god, there would be more intimacy between husband and wife, more time spent between parent and child, and more energy put into being rather than becoming. But we don't believe it. What we believe is that life is too short to waste in enjoyment, so we'd better hurry to accomplish something significant.

Receiving the World

The life we have been given—our bodies, relationships, talents, and accumulated experiences, as well as our infirmities, loneliness, lack of talents, and painful experiences—constitutes our personal world. Since this world has been created by God, it is a world full of dignity. Even in its fallen, corrupted state, the world we have received from God continues to be his mysterious and good creation. So we must treat our world, broken as it may be, with all the respect God's work deserves. All persons have dignity simply because we are the creation of God. Limited, fallen, and very needy, maybe. But as God's creatures we remain "a little lower than God," crowned with "glory and honor" (Ps 8:5). That has many implications for how we perceive ourselves, and thus for how we perceive those around us.

When we cannot receive our world as a gift, we are forced into the futile effort of re-creating it. We have to manipulate those around us into being what we need them to be. Wives, husbands, friends, and even children become functionaries who fulfill a certain role in the world we are striving to create for ourselves. We utter the forbidden words "Let there be" as we try to force others to live up to our expectations.

Creatures who exist among other creatures have no right to treat each other with so little dignity. Since we were not designed to be creators of our world, it makes sense that we are pathetically bad at it when we try.

To receive our world does not mean that we must passively affirm the conditions of our life, any more than it means we must affirm the conditions of the world around us. But it does mean we must accept that this, in fact, is our world—limited though it may be. In receiving our world we tell the truth about our needs, pain, and inabilities as well as rejoicing in the parts of our world that make us feel rather blessed. In receiving the world we find ourselves in need of the grace of God. That grace enables us to fill the needs that can be filled and to live with the needs that will never be filled. In either case, spirituality is found in moving from need to grace.

Author and Episcopal priest Alan Jones has written, "A human being is by definition a longing for God. The whole aim of the spiritual life is to keep the longing alive."[2] To long for grace is to discover life in the crucible of God's creativity. That is always a painful and yet wondrous place to be. The pain comes in having to encounter the truth about the loss of our dreams and godlike illusions. But mixed into that despair is the wonder of the creativity of our God. We know he is up to something. Something that only God can possibly create out of this chaos.

What will God do with our life? We continue to live with that question. We yearn for its answer. But to spend life receiving the mysterious creativity of God, well—it is enough.

———

THEN GOD SAID "LET US MAKE MAN IN

OUR IMAGE, IN OUR LIKENESS. . . ." SO GOD CREATED

MAN IN HIS OWN IMAGE, IN THE IMAGE OF GOD

HE CREATED HIM; MALE AND FEMALE HE CREATED THEM.

———

GENESIS 1 : 26 - 27

THE
INDELIBLE
MARK

3

When men and women look at their situation in life, they do something no other part of creation would attempt—they try to make sense of it. There is no clearer illustration of this than our preoccupation with the question *why*. Any pastor who has been called to rush to the emergency room has heard the anguish behind that penetrating question. "Why? Why was our little boy hit by a car? What possible meaning or purpose could there be to this?" Although we seldom find satisfactory answers, we cannot help but ask. We need to believe there is some order and meaning to our world, even if it currently remains a mystery to us. At this level, the *why* question is always religious. It is the lament of those who have just lost part of the foundation under their lives.

While this question is most loudly asked in times of tragedy, it is asked most often as a critique of the lives we have constructed for ourselves. "Why isn't this job more satisfying? Why can't I keep a relationship together? Why can't I do the things I used to do? Why aren't my kids making better decisions?" All these questions are ways of asking why life isn't offering as much purpose as we designed it to provide.

Social scientists tell us that the greatest threat to humanity is the discovery that life is meaningless. To live in a state of anomie, with all of the structures of meaning and beliefs crumbling around us, is absolutely unbearable to the human psyche. We can withstand almost any tragedy—devastation, loss, heartache, oppression—so long as we can make sense of it. If there is no natural explanation that satisfies, we look for a supernatural one. And if that fails as well, we're in trouble.

Almost in the Hands of God

There aren't too many things about being twelve years old that I remember well. But one experience I'll never forget was when the entire sixth grade went on a field trip to the great Ringling Brothers Circus. We squealed with excitement over the three rings of busy activity— tigers jumping through hoops, elephants doing handstands, and colorful clowns on minibikes. What I remember most is the flying trapeze artists. When they were ready to perform, all other activity stopped. This was the main event, and all our eyes were focused above.

A solitary snare drum paced out our heartbeats as the brave flier took off on his swing, let go, and began to spin through the air. No one said a word. Our hearts missed a beat while we waited to see if he'd pull out of the flips in time. I can still see that moment when the flier lifted his head, stretched out his hands, and was plucked from his fall by his strong partner. I can even still hear the reassuring sound of their hands and wrists slapping together. The praise of the brass band was drowned out by our eager applause. He had made it.

Much of the Christian life is lived out in that heart-stopping moment when we are dangerously spinning head over heels. We hope God will be there to catch us, to pluck us out of our fall. In the meantime we're hurtling through the air without a net. It's a hard place to be, although we're there most of the time—somewhere between having to let go and knowing that we've safely made it.

Security is always an illusion. At any time we could discover that the safety net is gone—the job, people, health, and money on which we have been depending could all disappear. Our only hope is for God to save our lives. To lift our eyes and find his strong hands of grace outstretched is the essence of Christian hope. The truth of the matter, though, is that most of us don't conduct our lives with the daily assurance that our hands are firmly in the hands of God. Most of us are living in the long moment that immediately precedes that joy. Most of us are still reeling head over heels through life.

We wonder if God will be there to prevent our fall. We don't necessarily expect that God will somehow come to the rescue and change the way things are. That would be great, but it isn't the essence of what we need God to do. We pray for the pain of life to be removed, but we know that frequently it won't be. Our loved ones will die, our health will fade, and eventually harsh realities will catch up with us. We can survive that, as long as God continues to give life meaning. That is what will catch us when life is spinning out of control.

The Myth of Getting It Together
Most people learn early to dream about how life will be. They believe it is up to them do something with life, something that will make them really happy. Some may even enjoy the pursuit more than the attainment of dreams, but just about all look at what they have constructed, or are

constructing, and claim this is how they've put life together. It is made up of the people, values, hopes, achievements and commitments they hold dear. But the hard reality is that life is going to take a beating no matter how well it is built. Not all of our dreams will be attained, and most will not offer near the happiness they were supposed to.

Like most pastors, I am frequently called upon to officiate at weddings. Weddings can quickly get out of control when the families knock themselves out to make the event a big production. I used to rail against these extravaganzas, but in time I learned that there is little I can do about it. Some families have spent years and years hoping and planning for this day, and they are going to be sure that it goes according to fantasy. The best that pastors can do in these situations is to look for moments to witness something that is truly sacred.

No matter how small or large the wedding, I have discovered that one of those sacred moments always comes at the very beginning of the ceremony. Without exception, after all the worries and preparations are over, after the bride has processed down the aisle, once it is finally just the bride and the groom standing side by side waiting for the pastor to begin, the woman and man always do one thing—they steal a glance into each other's eyes.

In those eyes there is so much anticipation. For just that moment, nothing else exists but their great hope for this marriage. It is as if between them there were a great secret that makes the entire production pale by comparison. They alone know how much they love each other, and in that quick look they are reassuring themselves that this marriage is going to make them very happy. I am moved by the intensity of their love. But that's not what makes my tears start to well up. When they take that moment, I take one of my own. In the few seconds their stolen glance affords, I always think about the families I will see when I stand in the pulpit the next day. I think about the marriages that fill our pews, about the couples who came to see me for counseling earlier in the week, and about those who are no longer married. I think about the parents who sit only ten feet away from the bride and groom. How very different they look. Behind their public moment of pride and honor lies a long history of private moments compiled through the years of real life together. How many times have these parents also looked into each other's eyes, not only with love but also with pain, disappointment, grief, and even anger? The amazing thing is that they are still married, still trying to love each other. The moments that make up marriage are far more ambiguous than the clear aspirations of the two at the altar.

If I could somehow show the bride and groom exactly what their next fifty years together would look like, would they still take these vows? Who knows? Perhaps it is a good thing that they can't see how reality contradicts the high hopes of the heart. But the real test that will determine whether or not this marriage survives is not the purity or intensity of the love that shows in their stolen wedding glance. No, the future of the marriage depends on what they will do in the host of moments that are yet to come. Moments that will not be so pure. Moments that mix how it really is with how they want it to be.

Not even the love that we find in the process of putting life together is strong enough to provide all the meaning and purpose we must have. In fact, love may be the very thing that threatens us the most, as it continually fails to live up to its promises. Hard work, finances, education, families, achievements, and even Christian lifestyles will also eventually fail to keep life together. None of those foundations is eternal. Sooner or later, every constructed life is going to come apart. That is because we are not creators, but creatures.

Dreams for Sale
When I was a pastor in Colorado, I frequently met people who had

come to that part of the country to escape circumstances that hadn't worked out too well. Often they came chasing a dream of starting over, building a new life in the mountains, where things would be more simple, pure and life-affirming. But there is a saying among the natives of Colorado: "The mountain doesn't care." This applies not only to the harshness of the elements that skiers and mountain climbers encounter but also to those who naively think that living off the land will simplify their lives.

Many get only as far as buying land before they realize they are never going to be able to handle the problems of construction, accessibility, hard winters, loneliness, limited supplies, heating, and scarce sources of water. There are always many five-acre lots for sale in the mountains.

One of my parishioners returned to the city after giving the mountains a shot. His property was particularly attractive, with a small stream running through it. On the edge of his land he posted a sign that read "For Sale: A Dream with a Stream."

It is hard when our dreams go up for sale. We get discouraged and feel uncertain of ourselves. What we do not do, however, is stop dreaming. This is one of the most amazing aspects of the human spirit. We just keep coming up with new dreams. Whether they are great or small, wildly ambitious or carefully circumscribed, our own or others', we are always going to have dreams. In part, this distinguishes us from the rest of creation, which simply does not imagine new frontiers for discovering life's meaning.

Rather than looking to their faith for an extra boost in this life-constructing process, Christians must tell the truth—that their tradition gives them no special edge in such a misguided venture.

In fact, the heart of the Christian faith couldn't be more antithetical to this attempt to put life together. Our gospel scandalously claims that we are never going to get life together for ourselves, and the harder we try the further we will roam from the God of grace. At the heart of Christianity is the confession that we are completely at the mercy of God to receive life and meaning.

Like the rest of humanity, Christians desperately need to believe there is meaning and purpose to their lives. Unlike the rest of the world, however, we also believe that we are dependent on the grace of God in Jesus Christ to discover that meaning. In Christ we receive a life, but we never construct one. If Christians lived with an appreciation for the mystery and adventure that are in store for those who receive life from God, they would certainly prefer that to their own smaller, more manageable dreams. How can wishful thinking possibly compare to the wonders of what life can become in the hands of the great Creator? The grace of God *is* enough.

Of course, to be in the hands of the Creator is rather frightening. Who knows what he will do? To be dependent upon him for the creation of our life is never a passive process. To receive his grace means we will spend most of our days struggling with God and agonizing over his intentions as well as rejoicing over the good creation as it takes shape. Thus, the confession that we are unable to get the life of our dreams is the first step toward authentic spirituality. As it places us in the position of dependency upon the grace of God, it guides the rest of our steps into spirituality as well.

Looking Again at the Image of God

According to Genesis, this dependency has been indelibly marked upon our souls. That mark is what theologians call the *imago dei,* the very image of God. This symbol of the godlike mark has been the subject of a great deal of theological discussion over the centuries, and it has been variously interpreted in the church's doctrinal formulations.

Typically, the phrase is used to assert the superiority of humanity over the rest of creation, which is not made in God's image. Sometimes theologians stand upon that premise to assert human responsibility for the rest of the world. Unfortunately, others use the premise to justify their abuse and waste of creation's resources. In recent years, still others have used this symbol to articulate a biblical doctrine that since both male and female are created in God's image, they have a created equality.[1] Symbols of such richness are subject to more than one layer of interpretation.

Whatever else it may mean, the image clearly serves as a constant reminder that humanity has been marked by God. I would offer the suggestion that this image testifies not to our superiority over the rest of creation but to our great dependence on God—perhaps an even greater dependence than that of the rest of creation, which has no hunger for life's meaning. What distinguishes humanity in creation is not moral superiority but the mark of a need—a craving to have meaning that is eternal and thus able to sustain us through the shifting tides of our years.

We've just got to know that there is meaning in our daily routines of getting kids to soccer practice, in worrying about airline schedules and the stock market. We have to believe our life matters to someone or for some purpose. We have to believe that or we will never get up in the morning.

This godlike mark, then, serves two functions. The first is that it is the source of our hunger for life's meaning, and the second is that it refuses to be satisfied with any meaning other than the eternal. All people experience the first dimension through their search for meaning and purpose. We illustrate that search in the various ways we try to construct life. Achievements, relationships, experiences, the things we collect— all these can be ways of trying to build our own lives. The hard truth, however, is that no matter how successful we may at first appear in these various pursuits, we continue to be plagued by dissatisfaction.

Christianity leads us to confront the second dimension of bearing God's mark, claiming we will never complete our search for life's meaning. Thus we are thrown back to our need for the eternal God. Nothing quite fits into the space in our lives that God has carved for himself. Nevertheless—and we must be very careful about this—to be thrown back to a need for God is not an excuse for us to reduce God to one more way we can put our lives together. Rather, it is to be thrown back to the prayer of sinners who can only ask for mercy upon our inevitably confused and misdirected lives.

St. Augustine described the image as the God-shaped box that exists within human hearts. One can try to cram other things into this box, but of course only God will fit. But in a sense even that is an impossible expectation. How can the great Creator exist within the limitations of the creatures? Isn't any picture that we have of God in our hearts going to be limited by virtue of our limited human capacity to understand God? Yes. The Eternal is never contained by the hearts of his creatures. Thank God. If he were, he would be as inadequate a source of meaning and purpose as every other thing we've tried to cram into the God-shaped box.

Nothing that we control or contain within our lives can be eternal or satisfy the hunger for the eternal, for that which is not merely dust. What Christians have "in their hearts" is not the reduction of God as another piece in the puzzle of life. Instead, in their hearts there persists a place for the worship of the God who is too great to be fully known. And that means that not even "finding God" makes the Christian whole or totally together.

The Eternal Thirst for Eternity

In the New Testament this point is marvelously illustrated by the woman at the well (Jn 4). Jesus encounters a woman who has gone through five husbands in her attempt to satisfy life's thirst. She has lost all esteem in her village; apparently the other women will not associate with her, for, contrary to custom, she comes to the well alone in the heat of the day. She currently lives with a man to whom she is not married, and she is alone in her journey to draw water.

This woman illustrates the depths of desperation and loneliness to which a wild pursuit of satisfaction can lead us. No one can hurt us quite like ourselves. Eventually creatures become compulsive about finding something that might fit into the God-shaped box and fulfill their fantasies of living without need.

If someone hasn't yet made as big a mess of life as the Samaritan woman, that may only reflect the effort to be content with slaking rather shallow thirsts. Day after day most of us join the others of the village in the common pursuits of going to work, taking care of our homes, paying the bills, and doing it all in a way that qualifies us to have a place at the well of social respectability. But eventually, even the good people of the village have to find their way to Jesus. What is fascinating is that, had it not been for the woman whose thirst was so great it could not be satisfied in respectable ways, no one in the village would have encountered the Messiah.

Talking with the woman, Jesus constantly tries to push her into a deeper understanding of her thirst: from the water to relationships, from relationships to religion, from religion to hope. When they finally get to her thirst for a savior, the image of all human hopes, Jesus then reveals himself as the one sent from God. It is for him that she has thirsted all her life.

Notice, however, that we have no record of Jesus' "fixing" her life afterward. For all we know she still has to cope with being alienated from the other women in her town, she still has to decide what to do about living with a man to whom she is not married, and not one of her divorces is erased.

Yet the promise is that the water of Jesus will satisfy her thirst. That thirst will be satisfied only because Jesus has taught her how to worship—"in spirit and in truth" (vv. 23-24). The woman does not "have" God through this encounter with Jesus. What she "has" is a new way of finding water that satisfies her thirst.

That is what worship does. It regularly rehearses humanity's relationship of dependence upon God, who is known in "spirit and truth."

There is no one for whom God's refusal to be captured by his creatures is more intolerable than those who think of themselves as religious. That is why Jesus had the hardest time with the religious leadership of his day. It's not so different today. Christians have much theology about God, many spiritual disciplines, and plenty of convictions about what God wants. So we quickly assume we have found God.

It would be far more helpful to claim that in Jesus Christ we who were lost in the destructive pursuit of satisfaction have now found the hope of forgiveness and redemption. We have found repentance and a new beginning. We have even found the image of God restored in our lives as it takes on the image of the cross. But we have not found God. God has found us, and in response we now find ourselves on our knees in worship.

Within Christian circles we see a variety of different wells that vainly promise to contain God for us. For years, many of us thought we would have God if we got our theology straight or if we lived straight. The arrogance of that is questionable enough, but for some it has degenerated further into a dogged commitment to containing God in their rigid orthodoxy, inerrant study Bibles, daily devotions, and political agendas. Others who are not so attracted to the dogmatic traditions have taken the charismatic route, where they can feel the overwhelming presence of God. These people know they have a hold on God because they can see his signs and wonders in their churches. In my own church tradition we have tried to capture God in our highly sophisticated dry theologies, in our deader-than-a-doornail beautiful churches, and in our prophetic statements on public issues. But all we've really captured is ourselves with a few exclamation marks.

More recently, many American Protestants have developed a fascination with more historical, mystical and Catholic traditions of spirituality. Dissatisfied with their religious home, they have begun to hitchhike their way along the road of the desert fathers, the medieval monastics and the contemporary spiritualists.[2] Some have tried with Brother Lawrence to find God in menial service. And then by carefully capturing the right words in spiritual journals. And then, failing that, in learning to pray by centering down and avoiding words altogether. Truly enlightened Protestants today enroll themselves in short-term retreats at monastic houses, where they engage in the contradictory task of being a monk for the day.

All this can be an ill-fated attempt to get hold of God. As Nazi victim Father Delp asks, "Could it be that somewhere along the way a portion of humanity strayed beyond a hitherto forbidden horizon, to a terrain where God has chosen to be absent?"[3] Scripture is clear in claiming that our hope is found in God's taking hold of us, but there is nothing in the Bible that promises we can grasp God if we only find the right technique, theology or spiritual experience. Most of the Christian life is spent in faith, believing that God does in fact have our lives in his hands, even when we have no sense of that.

Something of God's face will always remain hidden, for he has positioned himself on the other side of a line we cannot cross. This is the line that separates creatures from their Creator, those in need from the God who provides, those who have become lost in their desperation for meaning from the eternal source of meaning.

God has marked us for dependency. The true monastics knew that was true, because they devoted their entire lives to prayer, not in an effort to grab hold of God, but to humbly set the anxiety and hunger of the world at God's feet. That was enough.

It is not always apparent that those who borrow so freely from the monastic tradition understand this limitation. Not even contemplative prayer can be salve for the irritation that goes with bearing God's mark. We cannot be dependent on God yet capture him through spiritual practices. What we can do is look to the thirst of life as a humbling opportunity to worship God, who alone has the waters of eternal life both for us and for the anxious world around us.

The Freedom of Dependency

God could not allow the line that separates the Creator and creatures to go uncrossed. It is his nature to graciously seek relationship with his hungry creatures. Human need and divine grace met in the person of Jesus Christ, who came to us as God in the flesh.

But the bridge that crosses the great gulf runs from God to us, never from us to God. We do not travel through the cross to find God; instead, God has traveled through the cross to find us. The significance of this distinction is great.

For one, it means that our lives are rooted in the daily experience of God's grace. For many, grace is a cherished theological concept that plays a complex role in their salvation. Unfortunately, that's often all it is. The grace of God is not limited to theories of atonement, formulas for salvation, or schemas of the end of time. Grace doesn't simply mean that the Creator has fixed it so creatures can get to heaven—if they say the right words, live the right way and associate with the right church. Rather, grace is the embodiment of God in Jesus Christ, and so it is the reality of a God who has taken on our humanity. Grace is the daily source of our hope that because God has us in his hands, life has purpose, no matter how tragic or dull it gets. We are loved, nurtured, and called to a use in his kingdom. As recipients of this grace, we learn to walk humbly with God whever he leads us, no matter how many painful or confusing detours we may encounter.

Second, to claim that God comes to us means that we nurture our spirituality by receiving the grace of God, not by going after it. Prayer does not "work" because it somehow allows us to harness divine favor. Rather, prayer is the opportunity to tell the truth about our need for God. Similarly, the other Christian disciplines do not elevate us to a higher plane of living as the true people of God. At best, they are all acts of confession. Through them we remind ourselves that God alone is our hope for discovering life's meaning, purpose and direction. For those like myself who have spent so many years trying to get it right in the Christian faith, there is great freedom here. Undertaking Christian discipleship is not a way of getting life right. It is a way of confessing our inability ever to get it right, and that without the grace of God in Jesus Christ we would have no hope of leading meaningful lives.

In our church, as in many, every worship service allows time for the whole congregation to read a prayer that tells the truth about our need for God's grace. Offering that prayer of confession is one of the most important things we do. There are times when I look up during that prayer and look out over the congregation. I see men and women who are knocking themselves out to get life right. Tragically, that is the cause of much of the sin we are confessing. There are those who are trying so hard at work that they are unable to care for those at home. Others are trying hard to find exciting relationships and are leaving behind relationships that long ago lost their excitement. Some confess their reluctance to be disciples because it may lead them away from the comfortable life they have been trying to build. For others the prayer hits home when it confesses that "we have not loved as we have been commanded." They have worked so hard to put life together that there just isn't any energy left to love others.

For me, it is always hard to get past the words that confess my pride, my need to control, my refusal to live as if the church belonged to God. I think about the elders' meeting that didn't go as I had planned. I remember how irritated I became when my carefully planned schedule was wrecked by the week's emergencies, how angry I was when a staff member complained of being overworked. "O Lord, I have sinned against you and am in need of your mercy." These are the truest words I have said all week.

Following the prayer in unison, there is time for silent confession. There we sit, a church united only in our need for grace. Pastor and parishioner, wife and husband, friend and stranger—we have hurt each other and we have hurt our relationship with God, all because we refuse to see the hunger of life as a hunger for God's grace.

Then as a community of priests the congregation declares their pardon in Jesus Christ. We immediately rise to our feet and sing the Gloria Patri. After telling the truth of our lives, we are ready to hear the truth of God's Word to us. Then, having heard God's truth as it comes to us in Scripture, sermon, and sacrament, we are capable of receiving the call to mission that invites us to leave the worship service with a renewed sense of direction.

In other traditions the worship service is constructed differently. Ours follows a pattern that many traditions have used for centuries. It is certainly not the only model. It is important, though, that however worship is put together, it provide in some way for this great drama of telling the truth—the truth of our need to live by grace, and the truth of a God who is dying to give it to us.

A third implication of the journey of God to us is that it offers a new appreciation of what it means to be human. When we give up our futile search to satisfy life's craving, we are stuck with the confession that we are always going to be humans in need. In fact, that confession even allows us to make need part of the definition of humanness. It can keep us from denying our humanity in the hopeless effort to get to God.

Many labor under intense guilt because they cannot live up to all the standards that define "a good Christian." Rather than having a devotional life that flows out of an enthusiastic response to God's grace, large numbers of Christians are slavishly trying to arise early in the morning to get through a regime of Scripture readings and prayers before rushing off to the real life of the office, the school, or the home. Not only is this in effect an effort to buy God's blessing for the day, but it also implies an unfortunate dichotomy between the spiritual life and the real world.

This is not to say that Christians should not have a devotional life. But it is to say that a devotional can never be a formula for getting God to help us be more than real people who live in the real world. Time for a devotional life is vitally important if it comes out of the heartfelt longing to bring our world under the umbrella of God's presence. Sadly, we tend to get that turned around, thinking that if we just do these things, we will learn how to live superhuman lives. This makes the devotional life into yet another manipulative attempt to get to God. The fact is that God has already gotten to us in Jesus Christ. In Jesus, God came into the midst of common, ordinary, daily lives. That is how he comes to us as well.

When my daughter Lyndsey was in the first grade, she was asked to be one of the angels in our church's Christmas pageant. She and her mother spent weeks designing the most angelic costume they could imagine. Finally the big day came. After she was dressed, she came bounding downstairs in her white dress, wings and halo, crying out,

"Guess who, Daddy! Guess who!" Beneath the long, flowing white robe protruded her pink sneakers, begrimed by all the long days she had spent playing in our yard, walking to school and being the energetic child she is.

Those little sneakers marked the real child beneath the costume. It doesn't really matter how we dress life up, or how angelic we try to appear to those around us; the signs of our humanity are always sticking out in some way. Our heavenly Father will always be able to recognize us, because he has marked us as his own.

Christ loved the world so much that he died for it. We follow Christ to the cross by living in the common places of our everyday world as a people who really believe only God can satisfy life's hunger. Our humanity, complete with its limitations, its hurts, and its very obvious needs, will always stick out, in spite of our religious cloaks. It should. It is at the point of those human needs that we are best able to testify to our dependence on God.

The world is focused on the illusion that every need can be filled. For that reason the Christian's testimony will frequently lead to the cross of rejection and abandonment. But by all means, we must not abandon our calling by living according to the world's illusions of a life without need.

The way of the cross never takes us away from the limitations and hunger that are characteristic of all humanity. It simply leads us back to the world with the strange message that our limited humanity is the mark of our need for God.

It is enough. It is a great reason for hope.

NOW THE SERPENT WAS MORE CRAFTY THAN ANY OF THE

WILD ANIMALS THE LORD GOD HAD MADE. HE

SAID TO THE WOMAN, "DID GOD REALLY SAY, 'YOU MUST

NOT EAT FROM ANY TREE IN THE GARDEN'?" THE

WOMAN SAID TO THE SERPENT, "WE MAY EAT FRUIT

FROM THE TREES IN THE GARDEN, BUT GOD

DID SAY, 'YOU MUST NOT EAT FRUIT FROM THE TREE THAT

IS IN THE MIDDLE OF THE GARDEN, AND YOU MUST

NOT TOUCH IT, OR YOU WILL DIE.' "

"YOU WILL NOT SURELY DIE," THE SERPENT SAID TO THE

WOMAN. "FOR GOD KNOWS THAT WHEN YOU EAT

OF IT YOUR EYES WILL BE OPENED, AND YOU WILL BE LIKE

GOD, KNOWING GOOD AND EVIL."

GENESIS 3 : 1 - 5

CHASING
THE
LIE

4

Emma Bovary, protagonist of Flaubert's *Madame Bovary,* was disillusioned with how flat life had become.

Before marriage, she thought herself in love; but the happiness that should have followed this love never came. She must, she thought, have been mistaken. Then Emma tried to find out what one meant exactly in life by the words happiness, passion, and rapture—words that had seemed to her so beautiful in books.[1]

Emma's was a pretty common discovery. Few of us have found the happiness that should have come our way by now. Dreams haven't turned out as we had planned, marriages aren't what we had hoped, jobs long ago stopped offering fulfillment. Perhaps it is time to embark on a renewed quest for passion and rapture. Along the way we will hurt a lot of people, but none more than ourselves.

In the church we have a name for this quest. We call it sin.

What Is Sin?

Sin is not just the lies we tell or the games we play. It's far more destructive than that. Fundamentally, sin is that desperate act to reconstruct life according to a cherished image of our own making. In the course of our misguided reconstruction, all sorts of lies may be told—not least of which is the lie we tell ourselves about who we are.

The story of Adam and Eve is our story. Like them, we have looked around at the garden in which we have been placed and claimed, "This just isn't enough." As creatures who mistake ourselves for gods, we judge the Creator's work too slow or too fast, too dull or too threatening. In our desperation, we reach for something more, something desired, something demanded if life is to be as we had hoped.

For many like Emma, the craving is an addictive yearning for more passion and rapture than life currently offers. Others crave more security and predictability than they have in the present turmoil of their life. As different as those two laments appear on the surface, they actually stem from the same tree, right in the middle of life's garden. Our fundamental human anxiety is rooted in that which we don't possess—which we were never created to have. If God's inadequate work is going to get fixed, we think, we have to do something.

We have had some help in deciding to help ourselves. We are tempted. Temptation is always a lie that hooks us at the heart of our desperation. It's the very lie we've been aching to hear—that we can be whole. Temptation tells us that the thing that's missing, the thing that marks us as a people in need, the thing that lies in the middle of our garden, can and should be ours. All it takes is a simple reach.

The forbidden fruit represents different things for different people. Yet there are some characteristics that underlie all temptation. By looking at phrases of the biblical text, we can explore the nature of this deadly lie.

"The Serpent Was Crafty"

Playwright Henrik Ibsen tells the story of a visit to a mental institution. Surprisingly, no one in the place seems crazy. All the patients talk so sensibly and discuss their plans with such clarity that the visitor is sure they must be sane. He questions the doctor about it. The doctor reassures him they are all mad. He admits that the patients talk sensibly, but it is all about themselves. And then he continues:

Here man is himself to the uttermost limit—himself, and nothing beside whatsoever. As himself, he progresses full steam ahead; he encloses himself in a barrel of self; in self-fermentation he steeps himself, hermetically sealed with the bung of self. No one sheds tears for another's sorrows, no one considers another's ideas. We're ourselves in thought, and word, and deed—ourselves to the springboard's uttermost edge. . . . O yes, young sir, we talk sensibly but we're mad right enough.[2]

In the anxiety to cope with life's needs, the world has grown crazy with self. But when everyone is crazy, it seems as though being preoccupied with self is the mark of sanity.

Life can never be lived freely under such conditions. Actually, there is nothing as enslaving as our world's repeated message, "Be good to yourself." Commercials tell us that their product will take care of our need. Others tell us that our needs are best met through a certain experience or relationship. At times, even the church tempts us to think that first and foremost the gospel is all about ourselves. As sensibly or religiously as it is all presented, and as pervasive as the search for satisfaction has become, if the invitation to reach for what is missing has come from the asylum of a people driven mad by life's deprivation, it is crazy all the same.

When I hear a lie over and over again, it subtly takes on the ring of truth. The lie sounds so good. I want to believe it. Others believe it. Why shouldn't I?

Temptation cloaks itself as the truth. The serpent didn't say, "Eat this and get kicked out of the garden." Instead, it said, "By eating this fruit you will become as wise as God." Temptation typically deceives by appealing to reason, freedom, and the noble desire to control one's destiny. It almost never comes announcing itself as evil. The longer we listen to it, the more sense it makes. That's because all our lives we've been hoping what it says is true.

Worse, we know that we will believe the lie every time we hear it. Even though we remember that we've been deceived countless times before, and even though that often ignored voice in the back of our minds is warning that we're being deceived again, we don't care. We are determined to believe this lie because it promises a way out. *This* time it will work, we're sure. This time we will finally be fulfilled and made whole.

There may be 999 good trees to which we can go and find nourishment for our souls, but we pitch our tent under the one tree that is forbidden. We stare at it. We dream about it. We want so much to experience the happiness we know will come from this fruit that we are blinded to the good gifts God has already given us. We will gladly exchange them all, all the splendor of God's good work, for the one forbidden trinket he hasn't given us.

Forget the rest of the garden. Let it all wilt away. What am I going to do about this one tree that isn't mine—this achievement that is just beyond my grasp, this purchase I can't afford, this affirmation I can't seem to get?

Sadly, like Adam and Eve, we find that in reaching for the fruit that is missing, we lose the things that really mattered all along.

A middle-aged man visits the nursing home where his father lies in a coma. He tries to say, "I have always loved you, Dad," but the old man does not respond. The son drives home cursing himself for having waited so long. As a retired couple sift through tattered old photographs of the children, one of them finds the courage to say, "I wish we had spent more time with the kids when we had them." A young woman sits alone crying on her living-room floor after hearing the devastating words, "I am leaving." She wonders how she let another relationship slip through her fingers.

It is not until the garden is gone that we realize how little time we spent taking care of it.

Doubting the Goodness of God

What is particularly striking about the serpent's temptation is that it invokes questions about the character of the Creator. Had it questioned the *existence* of God, Adam and Eve may have found it easier to resist. But that is not the question that is raised. More subtly, the serpent questions the *goodness* of God.

Pollsters have found that most Americans believe God exists. They even tend to believe that God is good. What people tend to doubt is that he will be good to them.

"You have probably been overlooked." In fact, the temptation claims, "If God is so good to you, why have you been deprived of that which is missing? Obviously no one is looking out for you. Not even God." For some, the needs and calamities of life are so overwhelming that their whole garden appears ravaged. Others are desperate because their lives seem banal, predictable, and boring. These gardens may not be tragic, but they aren't particularly interesting either. At both of these extremes, as well as in most of the situations between them, there persists an unavoidable question. How could God have called this "good"?

Today many are desperate for significance. They want to know that the world would miss them if they were gone. Frequently this is the motivation behind their relentless compulsion to work themselves to exhaustion. Others respond to the desperation for significance by searching for relationships. Often this is what motivates people to come to church. They are looking for a place where others will know their name and care about what happens to them. So what does the church do? It passes out name tags. That superficial device ironically announces that we don't have a clue who each other is and can't be bothered to ask. People leave feeling marked as anonymous and insignificant applicants to community.

In my experience, anxiety over relationships is the greatest single cause of human desperation. We never feel more lost than when we are alone. But we are never more vulnerable than when we are in relationship to another person. We are desperate to find ourselves in others, and very desperate to make sure we like what the relationship says about who we are.

There are few things more painful to a pastor than when a marriage in the parish breaks apart. Divorce always hurts. Nobody believes that more than those who have been there. It is always a lose-lose situation. Everyone, including the pastor, feels like a failure. We wonder what could have been done to prevent it. What did we miss? How did it get this far? It is particularly difficult when two Christians try to untie the marriage they once believed God brought together.

Greg, who I thought I knew well, decided he was suffocating in his marriage to Jeanne. He wanted out. He tried to be careful and responsible in leaving, but how do you responsibly leave your family?

Looking around at how his life was settling out, Greg panicked at the realization that the commitments by which he had lived weren't offering what he had hoped. He liked Jeanne okay and praised her work as the mother to their children. "But the sad truth," he said, "is that there is just no spark left in our marriage." Every time I saw Greg he appeared more and more restless. He said he felt he had mortgaged his freedom along with the house. Life was half gone and he had more dreams left over than he had years to fulfill them.

Possessed by such fears, perfectly normal men and women will do whatever it takes, hurt whomever they have to hurt, to get hold of their dreams before it is too late. In their desperation they doubt God's care for them and can no longer live by their faith affirmations that the garden is good. Actually, faith is the very thing that is left behind as they venture out on the quest for a better garden.

Yet it is also possible to doubt the goodness of God while staying faithful. This is the option of those who are committed to God's work in their lives even though they really don't understand him. In one of the many conversations I had with Jeanne following Greg's departure, she told me, "It just doesn't make any sense. It doesn't make any sense at all. How could this happen? I was brought up to believe that if you work hard at the right things, God will reward you. I know I worked hard on this marriage for over twenty years. I have sacrificed, I have been a good mother, I have prayed, and I have always been faithful to Greg. I just assumed that God would take care of the rest. Now I am all alone. How did this happen?" How does it happen that when good people like Jeanne do everything right, they can still feel like failures? What does it mean when one does everything right and God *doesn't* take care of the rest? Living without answers to those questions is one of the most creaturely things we have to do.

It is important not to suppress the questions of those who are having doubts about the goodness of God. If I had ticked off answers and shut down Jeanne's questioning, I would have deprived her of her own faith journey and forced her to stand in mine. Such pastoral advice not only would have ignored the courage in Jeanne's ability to tell the truth but would have also been strikingly lacking in compassion. Besides, how did I know God hadn't let her down? Was my conception of God so airtight that I was certain about his every motivation? Being the pastor can brutally challenge my own faith.

God does not need my help to defend his promise to do a good work in the needy lives of those who love him. It is *his* promise and *his* good work that are on the line. The pastor's task is not to take away doubt but to keep it honest. Honest doubt journeys slowly through the anger of our disappointment. The disappointment is not only in God but, more important, in what we'd hoped he would do for us. If people tell the truth, they eventually get to the point of even doubting their doubts, as they discover a more compassionate God than they'd previously imagined.

We have plenty of biblical resources to facilitate this ministry. In the psalms of lament we find some of the deepest expressions of faith in the Bible. The writers of these psalms took God so seriously that they cried out in anguish at the way his promises were contradicted by the unmet needs of life. "My God, my God, why have you forsaken me?" (Ps 22:1).

The classical psalm of lament always ends with a reaffirmation of faith. In time, if they are honest in the journey of doubt, God's people will find their way back to belief in the goodness of their God. For they discover that God has found them even in their doubts.

> For he has not despised or disdained the suffering of the afflicted one; he has not hidden his face from him but has listened to his cry for help. (Ps 22:24)

We discover that what we really wanted all along was not to be whole, or to receive the life of our dreams, but simply to receive God. We discover his grace, his very presence with us. That is always enough. What more could we ask?

Doubt is not the enemy of faith, but its constant companion. The great biblical models of faith all had doubts about God's goodness. These doubts never betrayed a lack of faith. Actually, these men and women's faith in God's goodness was so strong that it had to take seriously the questions that seriously challenged God's character. If there had been no faith there would have been no struggle, only the nihilistic resignation of "so it goes." Faith is the prize of those who pass through deep waters and strain for a deeper understanding of their God.

Greg and Jeanne went different ways on a hard journey. In their divorce they began a process that is filled with pain, guilt, and failure for all. But he chose to run from God in a frightened search for a better life. And she chose to walk through the heartache of Greg's desertion with the God she did not understand.

Greg is on a road that has no end. It keeps lying to him, promising that happiness is just around the corner, if only he makes a few more turns. Jeanne is on the unpredictable road of faith, just entering the dark tunnels of abandonment. Until she sees that God has been traveling with her, none of her prior beliefs about the beautiful garden will make sense. Right now "they don't make any sense at all." The mark of faith is that she keeps telling that to the God she cannot see.

The desperation of those like Greg, or Emma Bovary, is born out of a yearning to live with passion. This is one of the more common human anxieties. Whether one is driven by the yearning for passion or security, whether one seeks significance in work or in relationships, or even when one has become anxious to live with a comprehensible God, it can all be seen as more fundamental anxiety over death. Death is the constant reminder that at any moment we creatures can lose whatever we are clutching as a source of significance.

"You Will Not Die"

When I first knew my grandmother, she was the queen of her home, full of dignity and honor. She ran the house. She had carefully reared three daughters, filling them with love and self-worth. She embodied the best of the words "mother," "wife," and "grandmother."

Now those days of running things are gone, as are her husband and friends. My grandmother was recently moved into a nursing home. Her daughers pretty much run her affairs. They pay her bills for her. They make sure she gets to the doctor for her appointments. They try to make the best provisions they can for her comfort, her nursing care and her limited future. They also worry about how much she is forgetting.

Although everything for my grandmother is different, she really hasn't changed all that much. She may even be more herself than ever before. Her ever-so-tender touch is still there. It just shakes a little more. Grandmother is a victim of a universal condition. She is aging. Soon she will die.

At either end of life, in the crib and in the nursing home, we are reminded of our essential human condition—we are a people in need. Only in the middle of life are we tempted by the illusion that we can fill all our needs. Death serves as that ever-present mark of limitations. No matter how much power, wealth or scientific sophistication individuals accumulate, the harsh reality is that eventually they all succumb to death. It is the severest mark of creaturely status.

In Genesis 2, God tells Adam that the day, or season, of death will come when he eats of the forbidden tree (v. 17). It is clear in Genesis 3 that the inevitability of death is a direct result of the refusal to live within limitations. In both chapters, death is a mark of creaturely status.

Only creatures die, and on this side of the Fall it is clear that all creatures die.

In some non-Western cultures death is perceived not so much as a loss as a passage back to life. However, most contemporary Westerners have great difficulty adopting this point of view, no matter how much trendy pseudo-Eastern thought is peddled their way. Some take great comfort in the belief in heaven, but that still doesn't make dying a pleasant experience. As Woody Allen says, "I don't mind the concept of death. I just don't want to be there when it happens." Most of us see death as the grim reaper we can try to put off as long as possible. Everyone knows that eventually it will come, but who wants to dwell on that?

Some caution that in removing dying people from our daily lives and isolating them in hospitals or nursing homes, we effectively deny the psychological reality death plays in our lives. Freud warns,

> Is it not for us to confess that in our civilized attitude towards death we are once more living psychologically beyond our means? Would it not be better to give death the place in actuality and in our thoughts which properly belong to it, and to yield a little more prominence to that unconscious attitude towards death which we have hitherto so carefully suppressed?[3]

No matter how sophisticated we become in denying our death, though, it takes its toll on our perceptions of life. The fear of dying influences our choices in life far more than we would like to admit. There was nothing as tempting in the words of the serpent as its promise, "You will not surely die."

We live every day with the potential of losing life, but it isn't just biological life we fear losing. Far more troubling are the ever-present threats that some cherished part of life could be taken away. Deathlike experiences come often, haunting us with frightening reminders that we are not in control of our own lives. Even those who are young and healthy live with the death of their dreams, relationships, and early expectations of how life would be. Long before they die physically, the old suffer grievous losses of health, family, home, and the meaningful days of the past that no one seems to remember.

Loss is the inescapable mark of life outside the garden. No matter how fast we run, death just keeps catching up. Before we know it, something else has been taken away. Until we get used to that, we will never be able to enjoy the gifts of life while we have them.

A couple of years ago our church started a support group for folks with cancer. Some in the group are in remission. Some think that maybe they've beaten it. Others are in the thick of the battle. They regularly submit themselves to the ravages of chemotherapy, radiation and other experimental treatments. They know the odds aren't good for them. Regardless of where they are in the battle, everyone in the group seems to have a perspective on life that is quite different from the perspectives of those who have not confronted a life-threatening disease. In this group, everybody believes death is for real.

Since none of them is pretending he will live forever, they share a few other characteristics. They play a lot more than most people, and they are quick to avoid empty but time-consuming commitments that deplete their energy. Ruthless with any member who complains of "taking on too much stress," the group demands that the complainer drop those entanglements immediately. They can smell manipulation a mile away and seem less encumbered by guilt than others. They aren't superhumans by any stretch of the imagination. They are just real humans who are under no illusions that they can beat death if they work a little harder at life.

By having to stare into the face of their biological death, these people are better equipped to face the inevitability of the death of their relationships, their achievements, and their many aspirations. As Ron said, "I've just stopped trying to figure out so much." Shortly after discovering he had cancer, Ron took an early retirement and began to spend more time with the people and things he finds meaningful. Like everyone else in the group, he believes he did not understand the gift of life until he had to accept the reality of his death. There is tremendous freedom in that acceptance, freedom we were created to enjoy, freedom for any who take seriously their limitations.

I believe Scripture teaches death is not what God had in mind for his beloved creation. Nevertheless, the pristine garden of life is now gone. On this side of its gates, it seems God seldom prevents things from dying. From time to time we all hear encouraging stories of prayer "working" to alter death's course, but frankly, I usually can't see it. We faithfully pray for God to change the way it is in our suffering world, but everyday thousands of malnourished children keep dying. And as if our own injustices weren't bad enough, natural disasters—"acts of God"—continue to haunt us. Closer to home, we pray for healing in our own lives and in the lives of the people we love. In spite of those prayers, things just keep slipping away. We are constantly letting go of something, someone, or some cherished dream.

Actually, there is very little in Scripture to support the dream that God will fix life for us. There are some magnificent stories of healing and feeding. Still, as far as I know, everyone who was healed once became sick again and eventually died. Everyone who was fed was certainly hungry the next morning. Those great miracles were never meant to make broken people whole. The healing miracles were offered as part of Jesus' ministry of reconciliation to draw the broken to God. What God wants, more than anything, is to love us. But that doesn't satisfy us. We would prefer that he fix us.

Pain and heartache define an individual's life as much as joy. If someone lost his or her painful memories and experiences, he or she would cease to be the same person. No one is helped by ignoring or spiritualizing away the heartaches of the past. The path of spirituality is found in accepting and even loving that which is broken and scarred, rather than in searching for a new wholeness. We will always be a people in need. That is how we know we are creatures and not gods. That is also how most of us find our way to living with God. The only prayer I know that always "works" is the one that asks God to hold our broken lives in the arms of his grace. Most of the time, that has to be enough.

"You Will Be like God"

It is a peculiarly American fantasy to think that one can somehow get to the "right" place in life. We devote a lot of energy to "becoming." Some dedicate themselves to becoming successful, or to becoming free, or popular, or thin—the list goes on and on. Scripture invites us to give up the obsession with becoming and work harder at "being" the unique creation of God by exploring the rich mystery that has been revealed in every life. There is enough unexplored mystery in life to keep us busy as long as we live. Judging ourselves inadequate, however, we usually opt for changing God's creation.

Many today think they can change their "being," who they are, by changing what they do. Our society claims that if we really want to "be" happy, we have to do something different. We are offered new products that will do it for us, new lovers to do it with, and new vocations to give us work that will make us significant. Behind them all is the common lie that what we do creates who we are.

This myth reveals itself most clearly when you meet someone new. After you give your name, inevitably the next question is, "And what do you do?" If your answer is, "I'm a dishwasher," the person responds differently than he or she would if you answered, "I'm a brain surgeon."

That is because we assume that if we know what people do then we also know who they are. Young mothers and lifelong homemakers dread the "what-do-you-do" question. Similarly, some older adults who are ready for retirement refuse to give up a job because once they quit they will no longer have a good enough answer.

We begin hearing the lie at an early age. When you were a child and someone asked what you wanted to be when you grew up, you were not expected to say, "Myself!" The answers we were trained to give were more like "a fireman," "an astronaut," "a teacher," or "a doctor"—all things that people *do*. It only stands to reason that when we become adults and discover that none of the things we have done have made us happy, we simply need to do something else.

In truth, doing does not determine being; rather, being determines doing. It is only after we have a firm understanding of who we are that we know what to do with life.

Only God can give answers to the questions of who we are. But most of those answers are readily available to us. They are written into our created motivational patterns, our personalities, our family traits and histories, our losses and our joys. Any good counselor could pull that information out with a few simple tests. Most people tend not to like those answers, however, because they add up to less than what they'd hoped. Most prefer to become "somebody special." So they look at the other options around them, choose a piece of fruit that looks particularly good, and reach for the new creation they are sure they will become. But after grabbing hold of the new life, they always discover that they are not a better creation but actually a corrupted one. The good garden always gets distorted in our re-creations.

To say God's work remains good enough in our lives doesn't mean everything that happens to us is the work of God. Like Adam and Eve, we have been given the opportunity to choose the things that will hurt us. And we can be hurt not only by our own bad choices but also by the bad choices of others and by the random visitation of diseases, accidents and crises. Life in a fallen world is frightfully vulnerable. From the first two chapters of Genesis it is clear that this suffering world is not God's idea of a good creation. He obviously had something better in mind.

Furthermore, to say God's work is good enough is not to say that once we receive our lives we cannot improve them. We are clearly invited to work in the garden. In both Old and New Testaments we are given exhortations to be diligent with the lives we have. But there is a big difference between self-improvement and re-creation. Self-improvement is the humble perspective of good stewards, while re-creation is a desperate effort to surpass our created limitations.

To say God's work is good enough only means that creatures can never change who God has fundamentally made them to be. The unalterable history a person has, the gifts and talents possessed, the relationships into which one was born, as well as the intimate pain, vulnerability, and marks of dependency, all come as the good work of God. The ultimate question isn't whether one garden is better than another, but whether we can worship God in the garden he gave us.

"Your Eyes Will Be Opened"

We are intolerant of innocence. Perhaps we smile at it in small children, but innocence is almost never desired as a personality trait for adults. Few would be flattered to be characterized as basically innocent. That is not to say they want to be guilty, though. Usually, we are most comfortable thinking of ourselves as floating somewhere in the middle.

The lie of the tempter invites us to experience both good and evil and then heroically choose our own way. His temptation equates innocence with naiveté, and who wants to be naive? We want to be able to say we've been on both side of the tracks. "I've been good and I've been bad, and through the hard knocks of life, I've come to realize that good is better."It's almost humorous.

Without really being worldly, most people expect themselves to know all about the world, but to have survived their flirtation with its evils. Even Christians wear the marks of bad choices proudly.

Nobody likes a person who hasn't made a few mistakes in his or her life. There is nothing with which to identify. This is reflected in the characters of modern literature, cinema and television. Heroes are no longer believable if they are portrayed as purely good figures. Today's heroes, if anyone still qualifies for that term, are always compromised, conflicted and ambiguous.

It isn't that we've taken to rooting for the bad guys. Rather, it's that we simply doubt the validity of such values as "good" and "bad." The postmodern society claims things are just never that clear. So innocence is out and confusion is very in.

The forbidden tree was called "the tree of the knowledge of good and evil." Why was that forbidden? Is innocence really worth the price of not knowing the difference between good and evil? In responding to these questions it is important to note that Adam and Eve did, in fact, understand the difference between good and evil while still remaining innocent. They knew that God had told them to take care of the good garden. They also knew that God had forbidden them to take the fruit of the tree in the middle of the garden. What they did not have was an *experiential* knowledge of good and evil.

The verb "know" in the Hebrew often carries the connotation of participation or even intimacy. Certainly this is what is conveyed later in Genesis when we are told that Abraham "knew" his wife, Sarah. We are tempted to believe that in *knowing* the difference between good and evil, we will gain a greater understanding of life. If innocence has to be lost in the process, it's easy to assume that loss is only a rite of passage in the quest for a suitable morality.

What could be wrong with wanting to have our eyes opened? It only makes sense. If we're naked, we want to know about it. Perhaps that will allow us to see our way clear of the vulnerability of life. Perhaps it will allow us to figure out how we can re-create our garden according to our own cherished image. Perhaps it will even allow us to do something about the terrible void in the center of our life.

The problem with this line of reasoning is that the loss of innocence does not make us wise, powerful or whole. What we receive in exchange for our innocence is not what we'd hoped. We receive the same things that Adam and Eve received—things that make us cover ourselves and hide from the presence of God. Hoping to find power over our vulnerability, we discover only that we are now ashamed of the naked truth of our lives.

In effect, the effort to find relief from our desperate situation opens our eyes to the reality that our situation isn't so desperate after all. At least it *wasn't*. In giving up our innocence to gain that perspective, though, we now know what desperation is all about. Somehow we don't feel as wise as we thought we would. Our eyes are opened, but we still can't see our way clear of anything. Sin isn't just a theological word. It is a description of how desperate and dark life can become outside the creativity of God.

One of literature's great illustrations of this is the character Paul Baumer in *All Quiet on the Western Front*. The setting for most of the novel is the western front of the German army in the First World War. Throughout the course of the novel the reader witnesses the painful transformation of Baumer. The fresh young schoolboy slowly gives way to a weathered soldier. By the end of the book, he has forever lost his hope that life has meaning.

In many ways Baumer is illustrative of the transformation that occurs to an entire nation that enters war confident in the rationale that soon betrays it. Early in the book the reader knows what is going to happen. Each chapter reveals only another wretched step toward the inevitable. We watch Baumer slowly lose his life.

Near the middle of the story, he returns home on leave. As he tries to adjust to the intimacy of his family and their home life, he realizes how far he has slipped from all of that—so far he cannot return. He longs for his lost innocence but knows there is no return to the days of his youth. He has seen too much. At one point, as he tries to maintain a meaningless conversation with his mother, his heart cries out,

Ah Mother! Mother! You still think that I am a child. Why can I not put my head in your lap and weep? Why have I always to be so strong and self-controlled? . . . Let us rise up and go out, back through the years where the burden of this misery lies on us no more. . . .[4]

He knows, however, that going back is not a possibility. All that he can do is continue to sink into the identity of an "indifferent and hopeless" soldier. By the time this tragic figure reaches the end of his life, the reader almost breathes a sigh of relief. Actually, Baumer is dead long before he is shot.

That's what sin does to our lives. It distorts our identity, values, cherished relationships and sense of meaning. In trying to become more fully human through the loss of innocence we discover, like Paul Baumer, that we have actually become something less than human. Even more devastating, sin destroys the intimacy we once had with our divine parent. On the other side of the garden we are unsure of who we are. Lost in our loneliness and confusion, we cannot find our way back. There is no going back.

―――――

WHEN THE WOMAN SAW THAT THE FRUIT OF THE TREE

WAS GOOD FOR FOOD AND PLEASING TO

THE EYE, AND ALSO DESIRABLE FOR GAINING WISDOM, SHE

TOOK SOME AND ATE IT. SHE ALSO GAVE SOME TO HER

HUSBAND, WHO WAS WITH HER, AND HE ATE IT.

THEN THE EYES OF BOTH OF THEM WERE OPENED, AND

THEY REALIZED THEY WERE NAKED; SO THEY

SEWED FIG LEAVES TOGETHER AND MADE COVERINGS FOR

THEMSELVES. . . . AND THEY HID FROM THE LORD GOD

AMONG THE TREES OF THE GARDEN.

GENESIS   3 : 6 - 8

LOST
AND
FOUND

5

My twenty-year-old daughter just received her third ticket for driving under the influence," one of the pastors confessed. "In our state that means she has to do time."

After a long pause, he continued. "It's bad enough that I have to take my only child to jail next month. When I get back from this conference, I also have to face my church board. Most of them are real sorry this has happened, but they think if a pastor can't lead his own family, he probably shouldn't lead the church. Right now I have so much anger I can't see straight. I don't even know whom to scream at."

It was a pastor's conference I will never forget. We were a long way from the watchful eyes of our congregations. After ministers get tired of impressing each other with statistical success, usually someone starts to tell the truth.

"I knew it wasn't going to be easy to be the first female pastor of our church," a woman said. "What I didn't count on was that the hardest struggle would be with my own family. I thought my husband and I had worked through the issues of my call to be a pastor. I was at the church a year before either one of us realized how angry he was at having to give up his job when we moved.

"Somehow it feels as if we're wrestling with this in front of eight hundred church members, half of whom don't think I'll make it. Frequently one of the older women in the church will politely ask me how I raise my family and serve as a pastor. They never ask that question of my male colleagues. There is a justice issue here." After a time of reflective silence, she went on, "But that just makes it harder to confess that most of the time *I* don't think I'll make it either. In seminary, no one told me how lonely I would be."

Next it was my turn. "My father was a pastor," I said. "But he worked too hard at it. We would go weeks without seeing him at home for dinner. It felt crummy to compete for his attention with God. Who was I to question what God had asked Dad to do? When I was sixteen, my mother called it quits and left us. My dad was forced to resign the church he'd spent so much time building. He couldn't cope with the failure. Soon he also left and eventually dropped out of sight. I still don't know where he is. What really scares me is that every day I look more like my father. I spend long days in the ministry. After a debilitating committee meeting, I usually get home too late and too tired to spend any time with my family. My best hours are always given to the church. That's not as much because the church demands it as because I feel compelled to give it. I know how this story ends, yet I can't seem to get out."

As we heard story after story, I gazed into the dirty dishes that remained on the dinner table. Stained and used up, they were ready to be sent away.

Looking Again at the Lost

In the pastorate I find it dishonest to tell Christians that they are on the right path in life, the straight and narrow, the road of salvation. More accurately, they wander on and off that road through most of life. The Christian journey can be pretty crooked. We frequently lose our way. No one in the church knows that better than the pastor. That's not because we have inside information on our parishioners. It's because from time to time we have to tell the truth about ourselves. The truth is that pastors feel not just needy but very much alone, lost in our confusion.

That is the effect of sin in our lives. The gifts of need that God gave us, gifts that originally were meant to tie us together, have through sin become points of crisis that pull us away from our most cherished relationships. What God intended as a mark of connection quickly becomes a mark of division and alienation.

In their created limitations, Adam and Eve were held together in a bond of naked vulnerability. Adam's missing rib now belonged to Eve. She was flesh of his flesh, bone of his bone, and their hope for intimacy could be met only in cleaving together. In their mutual limitations they shared a need for God's creativity. These imitations came as God's gifts, means to the authentic, vulnerable relationships humans were designed to enjoy with both the Creator and each other.

In sin we reach to fill those needs as if we could be gods ourselves. The result of this reach is not that we succeed in filling the created voids that can never be filled. Tragically, the result of our sin is that our needs cease to bind us to God and others. Now those needs become the points where intimacy is severed.

It's as if one of two magnets had been turned around. What was a positive has now become negative. What used to pull us together is the very thing that now repels.

Like sheep that simply cannot stay in the fold, we are compelled to wander away (Mt 18:10-14; Jn 10:11-18). We don't look lost. Letting ourselves look lost would be tantamount to calling for the Shepherd to save us. If we wanted a savior, we would never have left in the first place. So most of us persist in the lonely trek of keeping up appearances and coping with need rather than confessing it. As our fellowship of frightened pastors tried to confess, the faster we run from our issues, the more lost we become. In trying to model good parenting, just and socially concerned ministries, and dedication, we had discovered not only that we weren't as successful as we'd hoped but also that we were alienated from the very people we'd been trying to impress. It is unthinkable for pastors to simply confess to our families and congregations that we aren't very good models of the Christian life. Not if we want to keep our jobs. Not if we want to keep our illusions alive.

But the only way we can hope to keep our relationships is by telling the truth. And the truth is that our created needs are not mistakes that we must fix or overcome. In fact, they are our best hope for being bound together in loving relationships. The harder we try to overcome these needs, the more lost, and alone, we become.

In wandering away from God, we've lost whole portions of our humanity. We've lost intimacy, families, dignity, compassion, and the creativity of God—the very things that were meant to give us life.

The Loss of Intimacy

Perhaps there is no greater illustration of just how lost we are today than the pervasive lack of authentic intimacy. We are very lonely people.

It is important to note that loneliness is one need God obviously does not want his creatures to endure. When he discovered that Adam was alone, God formed another human with whom Adam could become one. The image of one flesh is not just sexual; it is also relational. We are created to live not as isolated individuals but communally. When our needs are brought to others and openly shared and received, we discover the intimate community we were created to enjoy.

When we refuse to bring our needs to the community, it is because we are afraid of telling the truth. If we tell the truth, how can we hope to be received? So we persist in looking successful, or at least appropriate. We hide our loneliness under pleasant discourse and "prepare a face to meet the faces that [we] meet."[1] Beneath the thin veneer of these pleasant relationships lies a collection of very isolated individuals who cannot even tell the truth to themselves, much less anyone else. The very needs that should have drawn us to intimacy have led us into loneliness.

It even seems that the more people there are around us, the lonelier we are. For a couple of years my family lived in downtown Chicago. I was always amazed at how lost everyone looked in the city. We shuffled busily along, almost as if we were running deeper into the loneliness. Every day I boarded the 151 bus that made its way up and down Michigan Avenue with its community of strangers. Crammed into that bus were many important life stories that were never told. We all knew the unwritten rules about avoiding each other's eyes. No one could stand up to announce the news of a wedding, a pregnancy or a promotion. No one dared tell the person in the next seat that back home a sick parent was dying. We never, ever, told our stories. We just rambled along, lost in our silence, surrounded by strangers, known by no one. I've never felt more crowded, or more lonely.

Although people tend to have many acquaintances, most have few authentic friends. In an era of transience, people seem always to be leaving our lives. In fact, we've gotten so good at saying good-by that

it's hard to trust people will be around long. In *The Floating Opera,*
novelist John Barth writes,

> Our friends float past; we become involved with them; they float on,
> and we must rely on hearsay or lose track of them completely; they
> float back again, and we either renew our friendship—catch up to
> date—or find that they and we don't comprehend each other any
> more.[2]

Most of us are sadly lacking in the experience of friendship. Actually that
isn't just because we move around a lot. More to the point, we move
easily because we have little to lose in leaving. We certainly are not tied
to people who know us well.

Our difficult experiences with friendships, however, pale in comparison to the difficulty we have with sexual intimacy. An insightful image
of the loss of intimacy in sex is provided in the film *Jesus of Montreal.*
In an early scene a disillusioned priest is caught coming out of the bed-
room of a woman in his parish. He shrugs and glibly announces that
he's not a very good priest but is too old to change. After he leaves, the
woman confesses to her friend that she doesn't mind: "It gives him so
much joy, and me so little pain."

In settling for "little pain" instead of intimacy, we make a sad compromise. We try to come to terms with our condition. This happens
frequently in marriages that are viewed in terms of "making it work."
Christian bookstores are jammed with "how-to-be-happy-though-mar-
ried" books. In many of them the principles of management, negotia-
tions, and pop psychology have overwhelmed Scripture's claim that two
who are in need must cleave to each other. The legacy of these advice
books is that we have taught ourselves how to live in relationships by
minimizing the hurt to the point of "little pain."

"You're stuck with him, so this is how you can jazz it up with better
sex, parenting, and money management." Nothing could be further

from what God intended.

In God's design for marriage there may be much pain, but there is also always intimacy. That is because in God's design we do not manage our needs, we confess them. Intimacy demands hearing and telling the truth, and it assumes that some pain will always be the cost of that naked vulnerability. Intimacy also recognizes that we will be inadequate to respond to the needs that are shared. We don't mend each other's brokenness; we just hold it tightly.

If people cannot find that intimacy in their marriages and other cherished relationships, they are never going to find it in larger experiences of Christian community. It is no accident that the woman at the pastors' conference who was struggling to avoid the truth with her husband was also struggling to avoid the truth with her congregation. As long as the husband and wife hid from an intimate encounter of pain and anger in their marriage, they were ensuring that there would be no intimate sharing between the pastor and her congregation. For one thing, the avoidance of the truth at home made it impossible for her to deal with the justice issues at work. More profoundly, the shared fears that were her best hope for creating intimacy at home (with her husband) and at church (with her parishioners) have instead become private fears. The result is a deep loneliness on all fronts.

In intimacy, one is really known and really loved. Typically people think they can only have it one way or the other. "Either I can really be known or I can be loved, but certainly not both. Because if she really knows me, she isn't going to love me."

So most of us knock ourselves out trying to take on desirable roles in other people's lives. We are tempted to hide the awful truth about who we are from each other and even from ourselves. We tell ourselves that the little lies are meant to protect the ones we love, but actually they are meant to protect us and to ensure that we won't have to go to bed alone. We think this is our best shot at intimacy, but actually the lies are slowly eating away any chance we have of really being loved.

The deeper root of this problem is found in our relationship to the Creator, to whom we are also lying. Until we believe that God really knows us and really loves us, we will never be able to find intimacy with others.

Most of us don't believe that. Not really. If we did, we wouldn't be so ashamed of the naked truth. We have to receive love in order to know how to offer it to others. Until we let God love us, as needy as he created us to be, we are doomed to merely coping with the loneliness.

The Loss of Family

Our loss of courage to enter into vulnerable relationships has its greatest implications for our families. Usually it is the kids who pick up the tab for our fears about loving. Scripture is quite clear about this. The sins of the parents are always visited upon the children and the grandchildren (Ex 20:5).

Most parents really want to do a good job raising their children. There are certainly some frightening exceptions, but by and large we take the responsibility of parenting quite seriously. Many of the parents in our church have shelves full of books designed to help them in their role of childrearing. We may disagree over the theories and techniques, but few of us dismiss parenting as unimportant. But we must always draw a clear line between *parenting* children and *creating* them. It is tempting for us to move beyond parenting to take on a creator's role we were never designed to fulfill. Parenting involves receiving the needy children God gives us and then raising them with all the love and grace we can. But we don't really determine who those children are, and we certainly don't determine how they will "turn out" as adults.

Proverbs promises parents that if they train up a child in the way he should go, when he is old he will not depart from it. Any Christian who has the terrifying responsibility of rearing a child takes great comfort from that promise. I suppose there are some fancy exegetical techniques that could explain why some kids grow up in good Christian homes but still depart from their training as soon as they can. But there is more integrity in wrestling with biblical promises than in explaining away their contradictions. In our congregation there are some parents who have done everything that could possibly have been expected of them, yet their children, so far, have not become very healthy young adults. Conversely, we have some kids who have grown up in abusive situations, yet it seems that somehow they're going to make it. There are no parenting formulas that ensure a child's future. Maybe, as the proverb promises, when they are *old* they will not depart from their training. Maybe no matter how far they run, that training is always going to chase them. In the meantime, however, for many years, it can sure look as if some kids are lost.

Paul grew up in our church. He was active in the youth group and music program and was admired by all of us. His parents were very involved in ministry and seldom missed worship. They did all they could to raise their son in the faith.

Recently, Paul was sentenced to a maximum-security prison for two drug-related crimes. After arriving, he wrote the following to our congregation:

AN OPEN LETTER TO YOUNG PEOPLE

I'm 21 years old, a member of the church, from a good family like yours, and I'm serving a seven-year prison sentence. I don't want to preach. I just offer some advice.

Don't use drugs! I began using pot, LSD, and alcohol when I was 14. By 18, I was using cocaine. The same year I was convicted for armed robbery. Guilty. Now I'm in prison.

I got expelled from college even though I had two scholarships. I lost my driver's license. I sat in jail for 13 months and now I have been promoted to prison. Not one of my associates from the drug days has bothered to see if I'm alive. Only my family and church friends have stood by me.

The effect drugs have on your mind is paradoxical; the less you think the problem is, the greater it is. Always. Don't even start.

See you in a few years,

Paul

Christians are particularly guilty of perpetuating the myth that if they are good parents, then their kids are going to be just fine. We hope that raising them according to our biblical values will ensure their bright future. That sounds reassuring. But if we accept it, then the reverse must also hold true: if the kids grow up to have problems it must be the parents' fault. In the misguided words of the disciples, "Rabbi, who sinned, this man or his parents?" (Jn 9:1-3). Jesus responds by clearly indicating that's a bad question.

The truth is that no matter how informed the parents are, no matter how much love, discipline, and Sunday school they give their children, the kids will still "turn out" to be needy adults. Like Paul, they may even do desperate things to meet their needs. We cannot control our children's ability to cope with life's needs, any more than we can fill those needs ourselves. The sooner we can recognize this reality about our children, the sooner we can stop trying to re-create them, and the sooner we will enjoy loving them for the fleeting years they are with us.

This is asking a lot. The hard part of parenting is not that the task is demanding, but that there are no guarantees. Unable to live with the injustice of that, many parents assume they can help the chances by simply trying harder and becoming more invested in the children's development. This effort usually backfires, generating more anxiety in the children than anything else. The kids grow up as junkies for approval and have to add that dependency to the burdens they will take into their adult years.

There is a big difference between loving our children and fixing them. In loving them we offer both affection and discipline, but we recognize our inability to fill up or do away with their created needs.

Only God can create the selves into which our children will grow. Many assume that God has only half-created their kids, and the rest is up to parents. So they spend most of their years with the children trying to fix what God didn't get quite right.

Having grown discouraged with the search for their own fulfillment, often parents believe they'll be happy if their children grow up to be fulfilled. This hope is doomed from the start, since we are always raising needy children. Needy children will someday become needy adults—too needy to fulfill parents' expectations. The net result is that the kids grow up to bear the guilt for the unfulfilled lives of the parents. No matter what they do, or how many of their parents' dreams they achieve, in their hearts they know Mom and Dad are not happy, and somehow it's their fault. Apparently they aren't good enough.

Working against our children's limitations undermines the fundamental reason for parenting. The needs that make the children look to their parents for grace, the needs that should bind a family in learned intimacy, become needs that have to get fixed. Not only can we not fix these needs, but in attempting to do so we are actually trying to remove the glue that was designed to hold parent and child together—the glue of being nurtured in grace.

If a parent does not offer a child grace, it is going to be very hard for that child to receive it later in life. Typically the child will develop the same compulsiveness from which the parent suffers. Such a child grows up to be not only needy but also, like the parent, lost in misguided efforts to find approval in being whole, successful and admired by all.

Perhaps this helps clarify the doctrine of original sin, which has always seemed so unfair. What did David mean by saying he had been "sinful since the time my mother conceived me"? Theologian Reinhold Niebuhr has suggested that the doctrine makes more sense if we think of it not as a biological taint but as a "spiritual contagion."[3] We sin because we are born into a disease that spreads from one generation to the next. This disease affects our souls and imperils us with the illusions of our parents. Before long, we realize that we are as lost as our parents were. Someday our children will say the same.

The Loss of Dignity

We grew up lost. Most of our role models were people who were also lost. In time, we get tired of trying to find ourselves. Eventually we settle into being lost.

When people begin to make compromises with the harsh world, they usually pay in the currency of human dignity. They find themselves giving up on joy and settling for security and respectability. They tell themselves that the dreams of their youth were unrealistic, that the time has come to cope with how it is. They begin to adjust to marriages that are unfulfilling, children they cannot understand and jobs they hate but must keep in order to afford lifestyles they really don't like either.

Many of us do not experience life as "crowned with glory and honor" (Ps 8:5), but we assume this must be normal. In our hearts, though, in our bravest moments, we admit that how it is stinks, and we're only kidding ourselves to think it's going to improve someday. As songwriter Bruce Cockburn has said, "The trouble with normal is it always gets worse." The adjustment to sin may get easier, but it never gets better.

One evidence of the loss of dignity in our lives today is our preoccupation with busyness. When Adam and Eve realized they had sinned, the first thing they did was get busy. Running behind the bushes, they began to invent both clothes and excuses. The harder they tried to cover their created vulnerability, the less dignified they became.

Psychologist Rollo May claims we are the strangest of all animals because we run fastest when we have lost our way. We are manic about appearing busy. The trick is to dance on the edges of burnout without actually crossing over into being used up. We teach this to our children, and we enforce it among ourselves. Our kids have to juggle school, music lessons, athletics, youth group, choir and homework in order to remain competitive with their peers.

As adults, we've learned to compliment each other subtly by saying, "You look tired. You must be working too hard." Nobody wants to hear, "You look well rested." Busy is good. It means we are doing all we can to find a way out of our desperate situation.

The world is thus perceived as something with which we must contend, which we must work hard to overcome. We are alienated from our former places of good work within the garden and now must endure "painful toil." Having lost the created understanding of work as caring for the garden, the contemporary worker tries to conquer it. What was once a created relationship of support between humanity and the world has become adversarial. Now it's just you against the world. You'd better hustle.

Our datebooks are crammed with stuff we've got to do. We wear them close to our sides like modern six-shooters. They make us feel secure. When setting appointments we whip them out and show just how busy we are, how powerful and necessary we have become. What we are really confessing, though, is how hard we are trying to fix our lives. The harder we try, the more broken we become.

Our society's most successful public figures have taken on a highly instrumental function. Fortune 500 CEOs, athletic stars and even leaders in religious movements achieve fame because they have made something successful. Yet this doesn't insure that they are particularly good persons. There is no good humanity, no dignity, when we evaluate each other by how successful we make corporations, teams, or even churches. Human dignity is precisely what is lost when we reduce the glorious creation of God to an instrumental function.

Esteem can come only from appreciating the worth of God's creativity in our lives. But that's hard to do, because God's work is riddled with needs that the world around us promises to fix, if we'll just work a little harder. Sadly, the harder we try the more enslaved we become, servants of taskmasters that can never be satisfied by what we do for them. The individual who is busily devoted to the success of these devouring institutions is usually on the run from something—usually from what God has created.

Covering the Truth

Most of us wear some type of uniform. By identifying with a group we receive identity, values, boundaries and a way of thinking. Best of all, we learn who the outsiders are.

Some of us wear the gray wool uniforms of the marketplace, others wear military uniforms, still others wear academic garb. On Sunday mornings we come to church, dressed in our Sunday best, and find the clergy wearing the robes of priests and scholars. Some go their own way, refusing to abide by the standards of a group, but ironically, they become predictable by their scorn of all other uniforms. Even free spirits frequently do their own thing in rather uniform ways. Beneath these many identities we try on lies the naked truth that we're all vulnerable and scared.

As Adam and Eve covered their nakedness with fig leaves, so we wear the admired uniforms of our day in an effort to appear more dignified than we feel. We conform to our group's standards and assure ourselves that if we look so good we must in fact be good. This used to drive Jesus crazy.

He is in the temple teaching. As people gather around him, the religious leaders interrupt. These are the teachers of the law, the role models who are honored for their moral virtue. They all have religious uniforms that mark them as good people. The younger guys are in front with the newer robes. These uniforms are the distinguishing symbols of their education, their conformity to moral codes and their social respectability. They are marked as people who have excelled at achieving dignity.

These men are angry at Jesus, because he has no uniform. He didn't receive their education, nor has he stayed where he belongs. He isn't home taking care of Mary, as the oldest son in a perhaps fatherless home should do. Worst of all, Jesus isn't impressed with the religious leaders' symbols of false dignity.

Bolstered by the trappings of righteousness, the Pharisees devise a test Jesus is sure to fail. A woman has been caught in the act of adultery and is brought before him. "Should she be put to death?" they ask. According to Hebrew law, she should. But Roman law forbids the Jews to exercise capital punishment. If Jesus sentences her to death, he is asking for trouble with the civil authorities. If he lets her off, he not only will be in violation of the Hebrew law but will also lose popularity with the masses, who always expect religious leaders to take a hard line with sinners.

The drama of this moment is overwhelming. Someone has thrown the woman into the middle of the circle. All around, people are shouting questions at Jesus. The disciples are getting worried. Then, to everyone's amazement Jesus simply bends down and starts writing in the sand.

We aren't told what he wrote. Some have guessed the Ten Commandments. Others speculate that he listed out the sins of those who looked so righteous. Personally, I think Jesus was doodling, just as you do when you're stuck in a long, boring phone call.

At the climax of the drama, Jesus stands up and says, "If any of you is without sin, let him be the first to throw a stone at her." Dead silence.

The older guys leave first. Perhaps they've lived with themselves too long to keep lying about their potential. Following them, even the young uniforms hang their heads and leave.

Jesus' response to the question of what should be done with the sinner is to remind us that we're all in this together. The desperation that leads some into adultery is the same desperation that leads others into donning uniforms of righteousness. There is no sin greater than the arrogance of those who think they are only partially in need of the grace of God. When we demand that God do something to punish the "real sinners," we always encounter his silence. During those prayers of judgment, God just doodles in the sand, waiting for us to either hang up or catch on to our need for grace.

Conviction with Compassion

Jesus never really speculates about sin. This isn't because he doesn't have strong feelings about what sin can do in someone's life, but because he always seems to be more interested in bringing healing to those who have been beaten down by sin. Jesus even refuses to designate who the sinful people are in his society. In fact, he blurs the line between righteous and sinner by caring for the adulterous woman, the cheating tax collectors and the Samaritans, yet denouncing the self-righteousness of the Pharisees.

While we champion this prophetic stance in the New Testament, we are intolerant of it in the modern Christian church. As one of the pastors at our conference discovered, some church boards believe Christian leaders shouldn't need grace. "If you can't fix your own kids, you can't stand in our pulpit." The theological implication of this dictum is that while we all may initially come to God in grace, the rights of leadership are based solely on performance.

No matter how many sermons that pastor preached on the need for grace, the congregation had no intention of offering grace to his family. Not that his people were malicious. It was just that they wanted to maintain the myth that at least their leaders could model whole and happy lives.

I have always been fascinated by Jesus' ability to hold together the two commitments of *compassion* and *conviction.* In his compassion, Jesus cares for the adulterous woman, saying, "Neither do I condemn you." But because of his convictions he tells her, "Go now and leave your life of sin."

Christians must always approach the world with those two ministries held in a firm tension. Compassion without conviction is trivial, but conviction without compassion offers no healing.

If we take this model of ministry seriously, the church is placed in a very uncertain position. Jesus will lead us, and our convictions, into the very ambiguous, confused, compromised lives of those who are the victims of sin and are in need of his compassion. He will even gather those people into his church. Thus, we must always be very careful about drawing too sharp a distinction between those who are righteous and those who are sinners. Jesus' concern was never to identify the sinner but to respond to those who were in need of the ministry of grace.

The French theologian Simone Weil often wrote about the spiritual journey. Her favorite image for it was Jesus' parable of the prodigal son. "It is only the prodigals," she claimed, "who find themselves in the arms of the Father." The elder brother, to whom the father says, "You have always been with me," undergoes no religious experience.

Weil goes on to argue that it is very dangerous to our spiritual well-being to live too carefully. We live too carefully when we assure ourselves that, like the elder brother, we have always stayed with the Father. None of us possesses God. He finds us periodically, and those moments of encounter are authentic religious experiences. But all who really want to know God have to come to him as prodigals.

Although we are assured of our salvation in Jesus Christ, the Christian experience is full of opportunities to discover just how desperately we need that salvation. Actually, that is the good news. If the prodigal had lived economically, he would have never found his way home to the father. The constant reminders of how far we have roamed from God make us all the more ready to receive God's grace—which, of course, is the only way we get back home.

The Lost Creator
Our losses of intimacy, family, dignity and compassion are all rooted in the one basic loss of life. We have lost touch with our Creator. When we play God in every part of our life except the "religious," we discover that it has become harder to recognize the true God. In trying to domesticate God to fulfill what we need, we find that our image of God is far from the sacred God of Scripture.

Mircea Eliade used to speak of a legend that was well known in the mountains of Nepal. According to the legend, in the cool air of a mountaintop a huge wax god sat in solitary splendor. Generations of villagers from the valley below made their way up the mountain to worship at the shrine. There came a time, though, when some decided to bring the god down from his chilly citadel and establish him in the center of their marketplace. He was convenient then, and worship was not such a bother.

But in the heat of the following days, the wax god softened and sagged. And the villagers realized that they could now make a few changes in their god. Those who thought his countenance too stern molded a delightful smile on his face. Soon the god looked just the way they wanted him to look.

In the heat, though, he continued to sag. Little by little, the people began to take away pieces of the wax to light their homes. Soon all of the wax—and all of the god—was gone.

When we mold God into our image and use him to fill our own needs, we soon find that we have no god at all. True worship does not bring God down into conformity with what we've always wanted him to be. True worship invites us up to a fearful encounter with the sacred Creator of our lives.

In both the Old and New Testaments, mountains serve as settings for divine-human encounters.[4] It only takes a few minutes on the top of a high mountain for one to know just why God so frequently chose this setting. High peaks are barren, intimidating places. People don't belong up there. There is nothing to protect them—no trees, no shelter, just the wind and the uncomfortably thin air. The mountain climber knows that if the weather changes suddenly, he or she is so exposed that death could come very quickly.

To stand on the mountaintop is to place ourselves in the hands of forces and powers we cannot control or even resist. Centuries of religious experience have taught us that we are most capable of hearing God when we know how exposed we really are.

That is why worship must have this sense of climbing a great mountain to stand before God, rising above the illusion of being in control of life. The religious need at least a weekly dose of this frightening encounter to keep straight the terms of their relationship with the Creator. Our tendency is to reduce God to the flexible wax figure that we can mold and shape according to our needs. With our well-rehearsed jargon about the will of God, our airtight theological systems and our simplistic prophetic stands on society's complex issues, we tend to pull the sacred canopy over life a little too tightly. And in worship we have to climb above it all, if a sacred, uncontrollable God is to be seen and heard.

To live with the Sacred is hard. It means that we walk with a God who does not explain himself to us. It means that we worship a God who is mysterious—too mysterious to fit our formulas for better living. It means that God is not our best friend, our secret lover or our alter ego. It even means that it is just as frightening as it is delightful to stand in his presence. Our creaturely relationship with God is one in which we are, at the same time, both irresistibly drawn to him and humbled by the grandeur of his holiness.[5]

For this reason, we often turn to other gods that are simply more manageable. The need to worship persists, but in sin we are sure we can worship something else that is not quite so mysterious. The problem is that our substitute gods simply do not satisfy us. That is because we have been created with a craving for the Sacred.

Why? . . . Into Your Hands

But our craving does not end when we find (or are found by) the Sacred. On this side of the garden we spend a lot of time feeling the absence of God. The search for our Sacred Creator is not easy, even for those of us who have confessed our hope in the atoning death of Christ.

This should not surprise us. According to Matthew and Mark, Jesus himself cried the lament of Psalm 22 on the cross, asking, "My God, my God, why have you forsaken me?" According to Luke, however, Jesus also said, "Father, into your hands I commit my spirit."

Much of the Christian life is lived between these two statements.

Without either one, the New Testament would not tell the whole truth.

After my parents got divorced and went their separate ways, my older brother and I spent a lot of time trying to figure out what had happened to our family. I was confused, hurt and furious at the turns life had taken. Eventually, I took to the road and began traveling around, trying to "find myself." But no matter how far I roamed, I couldn't escape the "why" questions. Why wasn't it working out at school? Why did I have no goals, no family and no future? And where in the world was God?

One Sunday afternoon I was hitchhiking somewhere in Oklahoma. An older black couple pulled over in their battered pickup truck and offered me a ride. The driver introduced himself as Stanley Samuels. He told me that he and his wife were on their way to the Ebenezer Baptist Church, where he was a deacon. The church didn't have a pastor, or many programs, or even many members. But that didn't matter this day. Everybody always showed up for "Fifth Sunday—All Day Singing— Dinner on the Ground." They asked me to go with them. I started to say I was in a hurry, but the excuse sounded dumb before it even left my mouth.

As we made our way down the country road, Deacon Samuels and I got to know each other pretty well. He asked me what I was up to, and I told him I didn't have a clue. He told me that he had just lost his job at the cooperative grain mill, and he didn't really know why. Things were hard, but he really believed God knew that.

When we arrived, people were milling around the churchyard. The kids were playing, and the women were fussing with the food on some old picnic tables. Deacon Samuels just walked around smiling, joking with friends. After a while I saw him stand tall and begin to hum "Amazing Grace." By the time he got to the end of the first line, everyone had joined in singing, "I once was lost, but now am found. . . ."

I started to cry. It was the first time I'd cried since my mother had left. Now the tears wouldn't stop. They felt warm and reassuring.

We all know that song. You know it. You couldn't forget it if you wanted to. It's in our pores. That song belongs to us. It tells our story. If you hear "I once was lost," you've just got to say "but now am found." When we ask "why," as we often must, the people of faith have just got to say, "Into your hands." I learned a lot from Deacon Samuels that day, although he didn't give me a word of advice. As I watched him, I knew that in the midst of losing his job, his security and his means of providing, he himself was lost by every standard the world uses. But the world knows little about the amazing grace of God, in which Stanley knew he was found. Through his story, I was reminded of the hope in my story as well.

Loneliness was only half of the truth. Through the fears, the pain and the hard questions, a glimmer of faith emerged, reminding me of the searching hands of the Father. I am found.

———

THEN THE MAN AND HIS WIFE HEARD THE SOUND OF THE

LORD GOD AS HE WAS WALKING IN THE

GARDEN IN THE COOL OF THE DAY. . . . THE LORD GOD

CALLED TO THE MAN, "WHERE ARE YOU?"

GENESIS 3 : 8 - 9

AN
UNRULY
HOPE

6

At breakfast one morning, a wife looks at her husband as he reads the financial page of the newspaper, just as he has done every morning for the past twenty years. She longs to yank away the paper and tell him she is just as in love with him today as she was the day they were married. But she isn't sure it's true. She isn't sure he loves her. She isn't even sure who he is anymore. She stares at the back of the paper that covers his face and under her breath asks, "Where are you?"

A young executive drives home after a long day's work. Once again he's running late. He picks up the car phone to tell his wife that he'll be a bit late for dinner but will get there as soon as he can. His little girl answers the phone and asks plaintively, "Where are you, Daddy?" Immediately he realizes that he'd forgotten all about her first piano recital that afternoon. After he hangs up, he looks into the rearview mirror, disgusted with himself. He can't get the question out of his mind. *Where are you?* He remembers how much it hurt when his own father missed his first Little League game. This isn't who he wants to be. It isn't who he used to be. "What happened?" he wonders. "Where am I?"

A recently widowed woman goes to bed alone. It is the worst part of the day. She has drunk a bit too much wine, in the hope that it will help her pass out quickly. But the grief is stronger than the alcohol, and the tears start to flow as soon as she lies down. Her hand slides over to her husband's pillow as she asks, "Where are you?"

Some of us are lost in lonely marriages, others in the blind pursuit of success and still others in their grief. We struggle to find a way out, but the harder we try the more lost we become. Sometimes we get so lost, we don't even know where or who we are. It would be good to have someone find us, to tell us it's going to be okay. It would be good to have hope.

The Journey of God

The Bible provides one vignette after another of the grief-stricken God in search of the creatures he loves. This great story of God's search for humanity culminates in the arrival of Jesus as God in the flesh. Jesus walks through ordinary streets and villages, looking for those who have lost their way. It is the end of a journey that began with God's first walk through the garden. Jesus' birth, teachings, miracles and death are all paraphrases of the Creator's great question, "Where are you?"

Since the hope of our salvation lies only in God's search for the lost, it follows that true spirituality must always exist within the ordinary and the profane. In God's search to find us, he enters every dark corner of life. Thus, our saving hope is not to be rescued from the dark world but to live in the darkness by the light of Christ. It follows that we can spend a lot less time praying for deliverance from how it is and more time asking to see the face of God in every circumstance.

The Birth of Hope

God's entry into the world was not what anyone had in mind, least of all Mary and Joseph. From all appearances they were planning on a relatively quiet life. Joseph wanted to pay his taxes, marry his fiancée and settle down in a carpenter's shop. Mary had been planning on this respectable, reasonable dream as well. But all those plans were shattered when Mary strangely became pregnant.

Our experience of God's arrival is pretty much the same. I am often impressed at how similar the ministry of pastoral care is to that of the midwife. People call upon me when something in their lives has changed. Maybe they don't understand it at first. Often they're scared and unsure of how the change will affect the future. In time, this disruption grows painful. A move is forced upon a settled family, a business fails, the last child leaves home or a loved one grows sick and dies. I stand by them through the labor pains.

Like the midwife, I have been here before. I have held the hands of others who screamed in agony and wished for their old life back. I know these friends will make it, but for now the pain is overwhelming. They want me to do something to take the pain away. But I can't. What I can do is tell them they will survive. I can even remind them that somehow God was involved in conceiving this new life. Before long they may even choose to embrace it.

The difficulty of the virgin birth was not originally a theological or scientific difficulty. According to the Bible, it was a personal difficulty, born out of receiving something we had not planned—a visit from God. This element of surprise, even unwanted surprise, is critical to understanding the Christmas story.

The sudden arrival of the Holy Spirit into our lives is never what we had in mind. What we had in mind was a source of hope that was a little less painful and permitted us a whole lot more control. We didn't plan on loss, embarrassment or failure. We didn't plan on not reaching our dreams.

The scandalous Christmas message is that the Holy Spirit of God has conceived something in our lives that we hadn't planned. Like Mary, we may first have thought it was our ruin. Actually, it's the only hope we've got.

Both Mary and Joseph seem to have a great deal of difficulty with the announcement of the upcoming birth, until they hear that it is the Holy Spirit who is responsible. At that point, according to Matthew, Joseph decides against handling the messy situation by quietly breaking off the engagement. Even more amazingly, according to Luke, it is also then that Mary stops her protests and says, "May it be to me as you have said." What is it about the Jewish understanding of the Spirit that made Mary and Joseph so willing to accept this incredible disruption of their lives?

Much of the church's understanding of the Holy Spirit has been shaped by New Testament texts. Yet the Old Testament offers profound insights into the work of the Spirit as well. The opening words of Genesis tell us that in the beginning, when God created, his Spirit hovered over the dark chaos, bringing order and beauty to the world. This same Spirit, according to Ezekiel's prophecy, would breathe life into the valley of the dry bones.

Devout Jews like Mary and Joseph grew up associating God's Spirit with rich creativity. They knew the Spirit would always bring order and beauty to that which was dark, chaotic and fearful. If it was the Holy Spirit who had conceived this child, they knew God was up to something that would bring hope.

Most of the time that is about as clear as it gets for us, too. We know only that God is up to something.

Life is rather ambiguous. Even Christians spend a great deal of time in the dark, confused by the conditions of our lives. But because we believe in the creativity of God's Spirit, a creativity born in the places of hopelessness, we believe that his Spirit will guide us through the darkness once again.

Do not search for certainty in life. It will not come. At least, not from God. Real spirituality does not give final answers any more than it gives us deliverance. Spirituality is simply the commitment to make our faith in God's creativity a part of the struggle with life's questions. That single commitment makes all the difference between those who believe and those who do not. As long as we believe God is up to something, we have hope.

Shortly before her death, Gilda Radner, the delightful comedienne, wrote a book titled *It's Always Something*. She began the book,

I started out to write a different book about my life as a homemaker. I wanted to tell you about my experiences with the toaster oven, the plumbers, mailmen, and delivery people. But life dealt me a much more complicated story. On October 21, 1986, I was diagnosed with cancer—a more lethal foe even than the interior decorator. Cancer is perhaps the most unfunny thing in the world. So this is a seriously funny book. One that confirms my father's favorite expression, "It's always something."[1]

The reader laughs and cries through Radner's account of her heroic struggle with the disease that would eventually take her life. At the conclusion of the book she writes,

I had wanted to wrap this book up in a neat little package. Actually I sat down to write the book with the ending in place before there was an ending. Now I have learned the hard way that some poems don't rhyme, and some stories don't have a clear beginning, middle, and end. I have learned that life is about not knowing and having to change. I have discovered life is filled with ambiguity. Delicious ambiguity.

Some poems *don't* rhyme, and some of life's stories are really hard to understand. They never turn out the way we set out to write them. There is just too much "delicious ambiguity."

It must have been striking to Joseph and Mary that the angel gave them two different names for their son. The first name, Jesus, means savior. The second, Immanuel, means God with us.

The pairing of these names signals a reversal in our typical understanding of salvation. We don't usually think of salvation as having God with us. We would rather think of it as our being with God, and as being saved from how it is. We would rather think of "the victorious Christian life." But in Jesus Christ God is revealed as the Savior-Immanuel, which means that salvation is not our ascent out of the hard, pain-filled, compromised conditions of this world. Salvation is God's descent down to the lost world that he loves.

Becoming a Christian doesn't save us from a blessed thing on earth. Jesus doesn't save us from grief or heartache or injustice. But he does enter every one of those life-threatening situations, that he might find us there. Perhaps that is really the only blessed thing after all.

As Joseph and Mary would learn much later in their life with Jesus, salvation is a matter of having our eyes opened to see that God is with us in this life. When we really see that, we can start to enjoy the delicious ambiguity of life. That doesn't mean living happily. Instead, it means to live with the full range of emotions, many of which are painful. So even for Christians there will be days of laughter and days of tears. In the words of the angel Gabriel, though, "The Lord is with you. . . . Do not be afraid."

Forgiveness

God's search for humankind is fundamentally about offering forgiveness for our Great Sin. Not just our list of offensive sins, but more profoundly our one Great Sin. In Jesus Christ, God forgives our sin of refusing to live as we were created to live—the Great Sin in which all sins have their roots.

Forgiveness doesn't just mean that God somehow erases the slate on which all our offenses are written. That trivializes both God and our Sin, and it offers little hope for the future, since we'd just keep coming up with more sins that would need erasing.

Forgiveness is first of all an issue of our relationship with God. This is not to say that we don't need to ask God and others to forgive us for the dumb things we do and say. We do. But the point is that God is more interested in healing the disease of our alienation than in merely putting salve over its many perverse symptoms. Our ability to forgive others and receive their forgiveness is directly related to our having received the forgiveness of God. God's forgiveness is the basis for all healing activity among creatures who hurt each other and themselves all the time.

The hope of forgiveness is that we are finally free. Ironically, though, this freedom comes only from our dependency on the Creator. Only by having a restored appreciation of our needs, and especially of our created need for God, will we ever be free from the enslaving pursuit of pretense. God has forgiven us for trying to be God, whole and complete, and has saved us from the hell of living as if we were in control. He loves us too much to let us destroy ourselves in the reckless attempt to create our own lives.

To live as forgiven people also means that we can stop trying to pay for our Sin. For those who live with an awareness of how lost they are, there is nothing as tempting as the need to do something about this mess. Our Sin of separating ourselves from God so distorts reality that we think we can accomplish our own redemption. But no matter how sincere we are, we cannot redeem the pain and the tragedies that stem from our Sin. The more we try to manage our Sin, the more sins we commit. Forgiveness is found only in confession.

The great biblical illustration of this dynamic is the dramatic story of King David, told in 2 Samuel 11. It begins with the words we could translate, "It happened late one afternoon." The king sees a woman of beauty he cannot have. Because he feels the need for her so acutely, he violates this limitation. Events proceed rather quickly. The story is told with no speech, no rationalization, no dialog, except for Bathsheba's terse words at the end of the first paragraph, "I am pregnant."

The cover-up begins. Drunk with the illusion of control, David moves from plan A to plan B to plan C, with each new scheme becoming more sinister and devastating. For a while the illusion holds together. Until, out of love, God sends his prophet Nathan to stick a bony finger in David's face. Then, at long last, David hangs his head and says, "I have sinned against the Lord."

Psalm 51 is David's confession. He begins by telling the truth of his need for cleansing from the sin that is ever before him. Then he claims in verse 4, "Against you, you only, have I sinned." David recognizes that the real Sin was not what he did to Uriah, Joab, Bathsheba or the rest of the nation—though all of them were hurt by his actions. These sins had flowed from his Sin against God. David's lust wasn't just for Bathsheba. Fundamentally, it was a lust to live as a god, without needs. Until that Sin against God is confessed, it is pointless to talk about David's offenses against others.

We are always closest to God when we admit how far we have roamed. I cannot remember how many times I have sat in my office and heard the tearful stories of men and women as they confess the lies they have believed and told to themselves over and over, the destruction these lies have caused, and their inability to do anything more than ask for God's forgiveness. In those moments I have often thought how much closer this broken spirit is to the heart of God than I am. In telling the truth about ourselves we are always better able to hear the truth about God's grace.

David's psalm of confession moves on to make a request:

Create in me a pure heart, O God,

and renew a steadfast spirit within me.

Do not cast me from your presence

or take your Holy Spirit from me.

Restore to me the joy of your salvation

and grant me a willing spirit, to sustain me. (Ps 51:10-12)

Having confessed our Sin, there comes a time to hear the hope of God's forgiveness. We are told in 2 Samuel that as David confessed, he prayed and fasted for days. Then he heard that the judgment of God has been satisfied—and he got up, washed himself, ate, worshiped and returned to his life. He accepted God's forgiveness and received a clean heart and a restored joy.

On the cross of Jesus Christ, we discover, the judgment of God has been satisfied. It is over. God is not the Divine Disciplinarian waiting to wreak havoc in our lives when we commit sins. Heartache may follow our sins as a direct result of what we have done, but on this side of the cross all of God's judgment is satisfied. What is still waiting is our acceptance of the forgiveness he offers. What is waiting is a clean heart.

Our hope is rooted in the event that occurred two thousand years ago on the cross of Calvary. Christ hung on the cross to bring the presence of God to all who have been judged lost and in Sin. We cannot read David's story, or tell our story, without being drawn to the hope of the cross. Remember that story? It happened late one afternoon. Jesus died, and we were forgiven.

The Defilement of Hope

Our hope, our salvation and forgiveness, is only accomplished because God was willing to be defiled in his search for us. One of the most heartbreaking experiences for any pastor is the discovery that a parishioner has been in trouble for a number of months, but no one has known. Perhaps a family is in trouble, a frightening medical diagnosis has been made, or there has been a serious moral failure. Just when they most need the grace of the church's ministry, some people withdraw into their pain and failure. Yet the loneliness only makes them hurt all the more.

When I have heard of these isolated, wounded members and sought them out, I've often found that they are ashamed of their needs. Some are even reluctant to pray about the problems they are enduring. Frequently, they will thank me for my concern and say, "As soon as I take care of this mess, I'll come back to church." That's analogous to saying that as soon as I get better, I'll check into a hospital.

Many of us think that we have to take care of our mess before we can confront God in worship. We come to church and find ourselves surrounded by attractive people who are beautifully dressed. We sit in a beautiful sanctuary, hear beautiful music and beautifully crafted prayers, and greet so many beautiful smiles. No wonder it can be hard to come to church when you feel anything but beautiful. No matter how much grace is spoken or offered in the sacrament, we often give the subtle message that worship is a matter of looking good before God.

Through Jesus Christ, God seeks us out in the dark valleys of life. "Even though I walk through the valley of the shadow of death, I will fear no evil, for you are with me. . . ." That is hard to believe, though, because we think it's pretty important to look our best if we're going to meet God. For God to come down to our lost, compromised, sinful existence not only would humble us but would also defile our standard of righteousness. What hope would we have of cleaning up our lives if even the standard was defiled? But in Jesus Christ, that is exactly what happened: the hope of righteousness became defiled. Although Jesus spent most of his ministry hanging around the wrong type of people, there is no better illustration of his willingness to be defiled to find us than his encounter with Pilate (Jn 18:28-40).

I have a hunch that somewhere along the line Pilate had said the wrong thing to somebody in Rome. The governorship of Judea was not a fast-track job in the diplomatic corps. It was the kind of job you got stuck with. Most of the time nobody was really sure who was in charge of Judea. Was it the high priest, King Herod, Caesar, or prophets like John the Baptist? The Jews had highly organized councils, such as the Sanhedrin, that tended to do what they wanted. The land was plagued with groups of political zealots who were always trying to stir up rebellion.

Worse, by the time our New Testament passages catch up to Pilate it is Passover, that annual Jewish commemoration of God's deliverance from the oppressor. Surely, someone will draw parallels between Rome and Egypt once again this year. But the thing that bugs Pilate the most is that the Jews have this habit of referring to him as unclean. Not only is he an unwanted outsider, but, since he was a Gentile, his very house is considered defiled. It's as if he had leprosy.

When word comes that Caiaphas, the high priest, is sending over a prisoner, Pilate knows he'll have to go outside to greet the Jews. Outside he asks the crowd, "What charges are you bringing against this man?" They tell him, in so many words, "He's an evildoer. Why do you think we are here?"

Pilate knows why they are there. They want the prisoner dead. That's the only reason they'd come to his house..

These religious pillars of Judea have great contempt for Pilate. They refuse to enter his home for fear of being defiled, but they have no problem demanding that he kill off their "evildoer"—whatever that means.

It's likely that these Jews have long forgotten, and that Pilate has never known, that years ago the old prophet Zephaniah claimed that the whole city of Jerusalem was actually defiled (Zeph 3:1-2). According to the prophet, the city's only hope is to wait for the day in which the Lord himself will rise up as a witness (Zeph 3:8). Neither Pilate nor the Jews have any idea it is that Lord who is now being defiled as Pilate leads Jesus into his home.

These days, it's rare for us to get too worked up about being compromised and defiled. We don't think we have any particular compulsiveness about maintaining ritual purity. But I doubt that is true. In the Greek, "defiled" has the connotation of becoming stained. Today it is still the concern of the religious to avoid the stains of the world. Some don't want to be stained by the world's values of materialism, its preoccupation with success, its lifestyles or its commitment to power. Others don't want to be stained by contact with the world's failures, its addicts and sexual deviants. Most hope that somehow their children can grow up unaffected by our world's social diseases, violence and bent toward injustice.

Religion, we believe, ought to do something about this mess. So like those who went before us to the house of Pilate, we take Jesus to the door of those defiled places and pitch him inside. We hope that another offering, another program, another petition will take away the things that could stain our lives. In fact, we are very concerned about ritual purity.

The problem is that God doesn't seem to share our concern. From the moment the Word became flesh and lived among us, the purity of God was stained by contact with a sadly fallen world. "God made him who had no sin to be sin for us, so that in him we might become the righteousness of God" (2 Cor 5:21). In other words, our only hope for becoming "right" in God's eyes is that Jesus Christ became defiled.

As a Jew, Jesus became defiled by entering Pilate's house, and as God incarnate, he becomes defiled by entering our houses as well. That is how salvation works.

The Holy God of compassion enters homes of people who try hard, but nevertheless are stained by love that isn't returned, dreams that are never going to come true, brokenness that cannot be fixed and failures they can't even admit to themselves. In some homes the stains are obvious. Others of us have been able to hide the defilement under a thin veneer of decency. Perhaps those with the obvious stains are most fortunate, because they cannot lie. They've been disqualified from a game none of us are going to win anyway. Our only hope is that, in Christ, God has come looking for us. When he finds us, he won't settle for anything less than empty and open hands. That is the only way we can embrace him.

This has some pressing implications for the church. If we follow the journey of Jesus, we'll find ourselves spending a lot of time with people we never thought Jesus knew. That is why the religious called Jesus an "evildoer." He persists in compromising all that is so clearly holy to us— our values, the institutions we've built, the positions we've spent a lifetime defending.

The wealthy will feel guilty to find Jesus in the home of the poor, and the poor will feel betrayed to find him in the home of the wealthy. Catholics will discover him in the home of Protestants, and Protestants will be surprised to find him in the home of Catholics. He will enter the home of the homosexual as well as the home of the heterosexual and will defile himself in the home of the pro-choice people as well as the home of pro-lifers.

Why is he there? How could he possibly compromise himself by going where we wouldn't even go? He is not there in solidarity, not to defend or support. He is there to reconcile us all to our God.

And if Jesus is there, the church had better be there too. The church had better always be a defiled institution.

Hope is always found where Jesus is found, and Jesus is always found in the places that need him most. "It is not the healthy who need a doctor, but the sick" (Mt 9:12).

As they bear the name of Christ, Christians learn to go to the places that are uncomfortable. You just knew that you and Jesus didn't belong in these places. But these are the places that need hope, the places Jesus is determined to go in his wild pursuit to find humanity and bring us back to the love of God.

The Death of the Hero

As we continue to follow the passion narratives, they provide more perspectives on the nature of our hope in Jesus Christ. Peter's experience during his Lord's arrest is particularly illuminating.

While Jesus was being interrogated in the home of the high priest, Peter waited in the courtyard outside. From where he was standing he heard them interrogating the Lord he had sworn to defend. He flinched when Jesus was slapped.

Suddenly, a question shot out, "Aren't you one of his disciples?" Peter hesitated for what seemed an eternity. He knew this was his moment. He thought, "For three years Jesus has tried to make something of me. He believed in me when no one else did."

The frightened but determined disciple dug deep and found something heroic inside. He blurted out, "Yes! Yes! I am a disciple of Jesus of Nazareth. If you're going to take him you have to take me too, because I would rather die with him than live without him. I am a disciple!"

The crowd was so impressed by Peter's courage that they asked him to speak some more. As the hours passed, this crowd that had begun as a lynch mob soon started to repent. Revival broke out, right there in the courtyard.

Later that night, Pilate came to ask the crowd whom they wanted released. All the new converts screamed out, "Give us Jesus! Give us Jesus!" When Jesus was released, he and Peter rushed together in a tearful embrace, as the Lord said, "I wouldn't have survived without you." The crowd was thrilled with what Peter had done.

But of course, Barabbas was not saved.

In case you're still in doubt, that is not the Word of God. As bad as it sounds, however, it is the word we would love to hear. We'd like to believe that when the chips are down, if we try hard, we can pull through. And that would be good, because Jesus really needs our help.

In pretend stories I don't need grace. I'm the hero who makes a few mistakes but gets it right in the end. In pretend stories everyone dies happily of old age. By contrast, in real stories people frequently fail at the commitments they make, not the least of which are commitments made to God. In God's story, those failures become the only opportunity we've got to discover hope. In God's story, we can't keep Jesus alive, no matter how relevantly we present him or how inspirationally we preach. That is because the place of the divine-human encounter is always the cross of Jesus Christ.

The authors of Scripture sometimes say as much by how they arrange their material as they do by the words that are used. Consider how John edited the account of Peter's denial (Jn 18:15-27). Jesus is asked about his teaching. He responds, "My teaching is public. If you want to know what I've said, ask those who have heard me." Notice, Jesus bases his defense on the testimony of the disciples. The scene then immediately shifts back to Peter, and we hear him deny his Lord a second and then a third time. The failure could not have been more dramatic.

Why does Peter fail? Is he a coward? Apparently not. Earlier that same night Peter went charging with a sword into the crowd that arrested Jesus. It's doubtful that Peter denies Jesus because he is afraid of dying. I think Peter denies he is a disciple because it is the truth.

He knows now that Jesus is going to a cross. From the start Jesus has been determined to go there. Peter has tried hard to save him from the cross, to talk him out of it, even raising his sword in an act of heroism. But Jesus has turned his face toward the cross, and there is no turning him back. Peter simply cannot follow Jesus to the cross. So he takes his place by the fire with those who have taken Jesus captive. The questions just keep coming: "Are you a disciple?" The truth is finally out: "No. No. No." This isn't Peter's moment of denial. It is his moment of confession. He is not a disciple. He never has been. What he has been following is not Jesus, but his expectations of Jesus.

On the cross, Jesus is determined to kill all of our hopes and expectations about what he will help us do. He will not help us accomplish the heroic, not even for his sake. What he will do is love us. If we understood the value of that, it would always be enough.

After Jesus' death, John does not tell us much about Peter except for giving us one glorious scene when Peter encounters the risen Lord. The two meet on a beach, and once again Peter has to answer three questions. "Do you love me? Do you love me? Peter, do you love me?" With each affirmation Peter begins to realize that loving Christ is enough. It can free him to receive life as an unfolding drama, and it can enable him to feed Jesus' lost sheep. Then, and only then, Peter is capable of accomplishing the things *God* dreams about—things kept from him by his own expectations of Jesus. Once he'd thought those expectations were heroic. In fact, they were too small.

In our church, the closest thing we have to Peter's misguided heroism comes at infant baptism. The sacrament identifies the child with the covenant of grace. We hope that someday, through an act of confirmation, our children will embrace that grace in faith. So a central part of the liturgy of baptism is questions that are asked of the parents. "Do you vow to raise your children as Christians, to teach them by word and example, and to bring them into full membership of the church by their personal profession of faith in Christ as Savior and Lord?"

Without hesitation, the proud parents always affirm, "We do." I am always tempted to say, "Oh come on, now. Who do you think you are?" The question deserves a pause, a gulp, or at least a "So help me God."

When new parents immediately affirm that they'll make sure their child grows up as a Christian, some of the older parents in the congregation just smile and shake their heads. They know how much humiliation is in store for these young heroes. That, of course, is why we are identifying their children with God's grace. In the sacrament, God himself makes a vow to be loving and merciful to this child. As with Peter, for us to expect something else is only to get in the way of that powerful vow.

No matter how many Sunday school lessons, vacation Bible school projects, summer camps or youth group meetings that child endures, none of it is going to ensure what only God's grace can offer. In spite of all our resolve to raise the child well, the mercy of God is the kid's only hope.

Giving Hope Back to God

To say that the mercy of God is our only hope means that we must live as if it were enough to believe in a God of grace. The only promise on which we base our life is that God will always come looking for us, because he loves us. If instead we are banking on God's doing a few things that Scripture seems to indicate he may do, we have entered into the business of making deals with God. That means we come to God only because he comes through on the prayers that happen to be important to us, giving us good health, success in our jobs and a bright future. But God doesn't want to give us a good deal. He wants to give us himself. Scripture contains wonderful stories of people like Abraham and Moses who are able to move God with their prayers, but we must remember that these are men who have already cast their whole lives into the unpredictable grace of God. As they try to get God to change his mind, they are usually wrestling in prayer over the character of God, asking that he be as gracious as he has revealed himself to be.

We are not called to be "prayer warriors" who have learned to harness God's power. Biblically, we "have been called according to his purpose." In other words, we are called to be a people who are distinctive in the world simply by their commitment to God's grace. That is the basis of everything we have to say in the church. In some form that message makes its way into almost every sermon.

Preaching is one of the greatest privileges of the pastorate. It is also one of the most fearful responsibilities. In all honesty, to stand before the congregation and proclaim "Thus says the Lord" seems a bit ludicrous to me. Who am I to offer these people God's Word?

In our worship service, the sermon follows the choral anthem. Without fail, during that anthem I think about the people in those pews with whom I have fallen deeply in love. I think about those who are overworked and those who have been worked over by the hardness of life. I remember the woman who has filed for divorce, the young man who is afraid he may have AIDS, the older couple that didn't want to move into a nursing home. The anthem ends. I make the long walk to the pulpit, begging God to use my words to bring some of his hope into their lives.

For me, the struggle to find God's word of hope actually begins early in the week, with the first look at Sunday's scripture. Never have I had to wrestle with a passage quite as much as when I was preparing my sermon for Father's Day one year. The text assigned by the lectionary was Genesis 22:1-18, which portrays Abraham's sacrifice of Isaac. On Father's Day!

On Monday, when I began working on the sermon, I found myself embarrassed by this ancient text, come to us from a very different world. Today we would incarcerate any father who was such a religious fanatic that he would sacrifice his son. By Tuesday, I was trying to spiritualize away the scandal of God's command to Abraham by emphasizing that, after all, this was only a test. God wasn't really going to let Abraham do it. But then I had to admit that the test is too great. There isn't a father in my parish who could pass it. When the unsuspecting Isaac asks about the sacrifice, Abraham merely says, "The Lord will provide." I hate it when I'm facing a serious dilemma and someone glibly says, "The Lord will provide." Try using that line next time you fill out a credit application. Hope has to be believable.

Wednesday I started looking for another text to preach on. "Too late," my secretary said, "the bulletin is already printed." Every pastor knows it's better to keep wrestling with a hard text than to cross the secretary. On Thursday, I tried to take my attention off Abraham altogether and focus on God instead. But what does this passage reveal about God? That he asked for the one thing Abraham loved more than anything else—Isaac. In calling the old couple from Ur, God had already cut them off from their past. Now he wants their future as well, and, significantly, the future he himself promised them. Who can hope without a future?

What kind of God would ask a father to sacrifice his own son? The answer, of course, is the same kind of God who would later sacrifice his own Son for the sins of the world. "That's it," I thought, "that's the angle we'll go with this Sunday." But you know, it's a funny thing when you start to tell the truth. It feels pretty good, and once you start it's hard to stop. I knew in my bones that the struggle I was having went much deeper.

By now I have learned that if there isn't at least a sermon outline by Friday, well, then I'm in for a very interesting weekend. I was getting desperate. I kept asking, "How can I rescue this passage?" But when I finally heard myself asking that question, I knew I had reached the end of my struggle. It isn't the text that's embarrassing. What's really embarrassing is that I would be foolish enough to think I should rescue the Word of God.

As scandalous as it may sound, the hard truth is that God asked Abraham to place his hopeful promise back on the altar. God wanted the promise back.

The New Testament writers also struggled with this passage. The author of Hebrews claims that Abraham assumed God would bring Isaac back from the dead (Heb 11:19). In Romans 4:18, however, Paul seems to put this passage in a personal perspective when he claims that Abraham "hoped against all hope." That's a fascinating line. Could it be that the old father was willing to hope in a God who was greater even than his promises? It is a hard thing to expect of us mere mortals, isn't it? Unless, of course, we trust God.

Most of us would rather trust God's promise of a blessing. As a people of faith, we are right to build our lives around God's promised blessings. Yet there are times when even the blessings in which we hope are not enough to carry our faith. We prayed, but the wife did not pull out of the coma, or the check did not arrive in time. In those darkest moments, when we have to join Abraham in the unbelievable walk to the altar of sacrifice, we hope against hope, hope against even God's own promise to bless us. It is then that we hope in God alone.

When a couple stands at the altar and vows to be loving and faithful as long as they both live, they make some pretty incredible promises. Will they always be able to live up to those promises? Of course not. They may remain faithful sexually, but over the years of their marriage their hearts will flirt with professional pursuits, with the unrelinquished demands of parents and with their different expectations of what each will provide the other.

The mystery of what happens at the altar is not that promises are made, but that each partner is believing in the character of the other who makes a commitment. Their love for each other is greater than their love for the promises they make. Otherwise, marriage is just a contract—an unbelievable contract. If later in their marriage they have to return to an altar, this time the altar of sacrifice, it is their belief in each other's character that will determine whether or not they survive their disappointed expectations.

Similarly, our relationship to God is not based just upon the fulfillment of his promise to bless us and bring a good work to completion in our lives (Phil 1:6). The Lord does, in fact, provide. But the issue is the sufficiency of God alone. Our hope is ultimately rooted in God, not in what he can do for us.

Hoping When It's Hopeless

The story of Abraham and Isaac has a happy ending, because God stops the sacrifice just in time. But sometimes God shows up too late. Then we learn the hardest lessons in hoping in God rather than his blessings. Then we learn to hope when things are hopeless.

We're told that after Jesus hears Lazarus is ill—Lazarus whom he loves—he stays away two days. Why doesn't Jesus hustle over to his friends' house right away and fix this problem? Later, when the disciples ask Jesus about this, he says that he tarried until Lazarus died "so that you may believe" (Jn 11:15). Believe what? Certainly not believe that

Jesus saves the day. It is too late for that. Lazarus is dead. Perhaps Jesus is inviting his disciples to believe simply in God, and not in what he will do.

This same lesson is given in the death of Jairus' daughter (Mk 5:21-43). Jairus has done pretty well for himself. He is a ruler in the synagogue. It isn't a big position under one of the tall steeples of Jerusalem, but it's a good start. To have that job means he's probably the most influential person in his town. He explains God to everyone else. He is educated, a family man and well esteemed.

But one day his daughter gets sick—really sick. Nothing gets to a parent quite like a sick child. You feel so helpless that you would do anything to make the child well again. Jairus' little girl is only twelve years old. I've seen this same scene in hospitals too many times. When the dying girl reaches out her arms and says, "Daddy, it hurts," Jairus just about falls apart. It doesn't make any difference how powerful he is now. He can't do a thing to save his daughter, except invite Jesus to visit his home. In making that invitation, the ruler is willing to sacrifice everything that has kept Jesus away from him. He'll give up all he has accomplished to save his own life in the hope that Jesus will come home with him, touch his daughter and make her well.

By this time the synagogue has already taken a public position on Jesus, calling him a false messiah, an impostor. If Jairus is going to have any kind of future in his community, if he is ever going to make it to the big brick synagogues of Jerusalem, he has to keep the people away from Jesus. But the opening scene of this story finds Jairus on his knees before Jesus, begging him to come to the ruler's house. His little girl is dying, he pleads. If Jesus hurries, he can touch her and make her well.

Throughout the Gospels, most people who come to Jesus come out of a sense of need. They come when there is no other reason for hope, because all the other things they have going for themselves have let them down. Like Jairus, we all have something going for us—reputation, money, education, beauty, talent, family background or the ability to work hard. We don't come to Jesus because we are succeeding so well with these things. We come because they have failed to make us hopeful about a particular need we're experiencing. Maybe Jesus will help.

As Jesus starts to make his way toward Jairus' house, the crowd grows. People are pushing and shoving to get close. If Jairus can approach Jesus, it must be okay for them to seek a miracle or two from him as well. All of sudden Jesus stops the parade. He looks at the disciples and asks, "Who touched me?" The disciples are amazed at that question. "Who touched you? Jesus, half of Galilee is trying to grab you, and you ask who touched you?" But Jesus has to know.

Like the crowd, we are tempted to push our way to Jesus and grab a little bit of grace before it's too late. That doesn't interest Jesus too much. But he stops for a woman who has nothing else to lean upon and so she has reached out to touch the hem of grace as it passes by. Jesus is so overcome with this demonstration of belief in him that he has to stop the parade. He offers healing to this humble woman, who, in contrast to the demanding crowd, is afraid she has asked too much of Jesus.

Meanwhile, Jairus is going nuts. You can imagine him hopping from one foot to another, thinking, "Come on! This woman has a chronic problem. She's been sick a long time. She'll be sick tomorrow, but soon my daughter will be dead." The ruler has to wait while the healer takes care of a nobody.

Sure enough, just as Jairus finally gets the show back on the road, someone from home shows up to say, "It's too late, Jairus. She's gone."

The despair of that moment is overwhelming. It is too late. Jesus didn't hurry.

Jesus is not the God who comes heroically in the nick of time to save us from the fulfillment of our greatest fears. He doesn't do that for us any more than his Father did it for him on the cross. Rather, Jesus is the God who shows up at the places of death after the nick of time has come and gone, after hope has turned into despair, after the improbable has become the impossible.

Our saving hope is not that we are spared from experiencing the pain of loss. Jesus never hurries to save us from that. Our hope is simply in Jesus himself, who is greater than that for which we had hoped. We had hoped to be spared the loss. It never occurred to Jairus, or the family and friends of Lazarus, that Jesus could defeat the power of death. It usually doesn't occur to us either.

When Jesus overhears the bad news Jairus receives, he says, "Don't be afraid; just believe." Again, believe what? That a loss will be avoided? No. Simply believe in Jesus.

When we hope in God alone, we give up the illusion that we can control his creativity in our lives. In being freed from that illusion, we discover our hope has become anchored in the Creator, who is still about the work of bringing beauty and order to that which is dark and chaotic. The New Testament is clear in claiming that our hope is found in the resurrection of Christ. Yet Jesus can arrive with resurrection hope only in the places of loss and death. Our hope makes no sense until we give up on both our heroism and God's.

They get to the house. Jesus throws out all the mourners who make their living off people's fear of death and who laugh at his offer of hope for the dead. In the intimacy of a family circle, he says, "Talitha kuom! Little girl, get up!"

Now I would have expected the story to end with someone throwing open the windows and screaming out, "Hey, he did it again! He pulled off another one!" Actually, it ends with Jesus saying, "Tell no one about this." Here we find a deeper side of Jesus, a side that goes beyond the miracle worker who heals and feeds. This is the portrayal of Jesus as the victor over death.

That is not a very popular image of Jesus. Not really. In John's gospel, it is after Jesus raises Lazarus from the dead that the rulers begin discussing how to destroy him. Most people can handle a Jesus who helps us out from time to time, or who offers a little charity to those who are down on their luck. But do we really want a Jesus who is stronger than death? That would mean he is uncontrollable. It would mean that we are hoping in a God who is not as focused as we in fending off our greatest fears, our losses and deathlike experiences.

It might even mean that we have to experience our ruin to find our salvation.

———

THE MAN SAID, "THE WOMAN YOU PUT HERE WITH ME—

SHE GAVE ME SOME FRUIT FROM THE TREE,

AND I ATE IT." THEN THE LORD GOD SAID TO THE WOMAN,

"WHAT IS THIS YOU HAVE DONE?" THE WOMAN SAID,

"THE SERPENT DECEIVED ME, AND I ATE."

GENESIS 3 : 12 - 13

TO THE WOMAN [THE LORD] SAID, "I WILL GREATLY

INCREASE YOUR PAINS IN CHILDBEARING; WITH

PAIN YOU WILL GIVE BIRTH TO CHILDREN. . . ." TO ADAM HE

SAID, ". . . BY THE SWEAT OF YOUR BROW YOU

WILL EAT YOUR FOOD UNTIL YOU RETURN TO THE

GROUND, SINCE FROM IT YOU WERE TAKEN; FOR DUST YOU

ARE AND TO DUST YOU WILL RETURN." ADAM

NAMED HIS WIFE EVE, BECAUSE SHE WOULD BECOME THE

MOTHER OF ALL THE LIVING.

GENESIS 3 : 16 - 17 , 19 - 20

A FAMILY
OF
GRACE

7

When I step into the pulpit on any given Sunday I assume that at least 25 per cent of those who face me have already been hurt that morning by a family member. Many of my colleagues claim this estimate is low. Quite likely, a woman or child was even physically abused. Nowhere is the brokenness of life felt more severely than in our families. And that includes Christian families.[1] I have accompanied many of our parishioners as they journeyed through their anger at what families did to them and didn't do for them. Some make it to forgiveness. These people have then been able to accept their families with thankfulness, but no longer with illusions.

In fact, it seems our ability to love our families authentically is directly related to the degree to which we've told the truth about their limitations. When we see our family members not as gods but as flawed creatures, it is easier to make our way to forgiveness and acceptance. But the first step, telling the truth about how much pain these gods have created, is very hard. We would rather pretend things are just fine.

The more I have seen these family dynamics up close, the more convinced I have become that family is one of the best descriptions we have of the Christian church.[2]

Some may wonder whether this description of the church is as helpful as it once was. Formerly, families were secure and stable. Today, the family is under assault. Many of us are doing all we can to keep families together, while at the same time learning the truth about how dysfunctional and hurtful they can be. With the family in so much trouble, does it still make sense to refer to the church as the family of God? Yes— and now more than ever. This is not because the church necessarily demonstrates a clear, loving alternative to families in crises. To the contrary, it is because we understand the family to be *in trouble* that the image of family fits the church better than it ever has before.

The Family in Crisis

Since it is composed of at least two or three humans, the church will always be a family in crisis. This is not primarily because the members of the church constantly bicker, complain and threaten to split the family apart. They do, but that is not why we are in crisis. Our troubles are more deeply rooted in the personal crises of individuals within the church. Our complaints and divisions are only ways of acting out this personal anxiety.

The emotional processes of early family life are unavoidably transferred to the relational life of the church. This happens because the members of the church have been more influenced by their biological families than anything else. Churches derive their personalities, deci-sion-making techniques, leadership styles and expectations for relation-ships from the collection of family dynamics that are represented.[3] The church, in fact, becomes its own kind of family. To the degree that its members come from dysfunctional families, the church takes on the characteristics of a dysfunctional family as well. How could that be avoided?

Like all families, the members of the church are far more interrelated than they care to admit. The dynamics of any family life demand that we all hurt when one hurts, we all stumble when one falls, and the sin of the one infects the rest. The point is not that we should all have greater empathy for those who are in trouble. I guess that is true, but it misses the point of the biblical images of the family. The Bible calls the church a family not just to say that we should take care of each other but, more profoundly, to emphasize that the identity of every member is rooted in the dynamics of shared relationships.

The family tells us who we are. That is every bit as true for the church as it is for our families of origin. This means the church needs to spend less time dreaming about what it wants to be and much more time telling the truth about its strange and often hurtful life as a family.

My first position out of seminary was as a pastor to college students in Colorado Springs. I took the position with a determination to create an attractive community. I was loaded with dreams of what our group could become. With an almost reckless commitment, I threw myself into the challenge of making this college fellowship so appealing the stu-dents would be standing in line to join us.

One summer the students talked me into taking them to a Christian rock concert at the Red Rocks Amphitheater, which is built into the mountains just outside Denver. I had never been much of a dancer and hadn't been particularly interested in Christian rock, but I desperately wanted to relate to the students and was willing to try anything to that end.

The group that was playing that night was hot. They had the entire audience on their feet, singing and dancing in the aisles. Well, almost the entire audience. I couldn't decide whether I should just keep looking foolish, standing quietly among thousands who were having such a good time, or whether I should try to dance and look even more foolish. I cursed the years I'd spent in libraries. Finally I gave up and told the students I would meet them back at the bus when the concert was over.

I decided to go to the back of the amphitheater, where I could watch all of the excitement with detachment. I felt deeply discouraged to be an outsider, unable to participate in the culture of my students. How could I create a great fellowship for students when I was such a nerd?

After I collapsed into a seat at the back, I noticed a group of disabled adults. Many of them seemed mentally disabled, others had rather severe physical disabilities, and some obviously had both. But they all were having a great time at the concert. Those who could sing and dance were doing so with a wonderful abandon. Those who needed to lean on someone else did so happily. I thought how nice it was of someone to bring these handicapped people to the concert. The rest of the night I couldn't take my eyes off them as they sang, laughed and held each other.

After the band announced that they were about to perform the last song, the little group decided they should get started on their way home. To my surprise, they had no chaperon. They were there alone— together. I watched them slowly make their way down the back stairs into the darkness, still singing and laughing, still holding onto each other as they journeyed home.

It was all I could do to keep from screaming, "Wait up! Please! I belong in your group. I too am disabled." It would be so good to have that in the open, not to worry about how I look, to give up pretending I'm whole.

That night I resolved I would stop trying to create a beautiful fellowship. The fact is, we have all been disabled by life, and some of the greatest disabilities are even God-created limitations. The Christian family emerges not by trying to overcome its needs but by openly confessing them and then finding the freedom to lean on each other as we all make our way through the dark. As long as we are leaning on each other, we can even sing and dance.

But first, we have to tell the truth—that we are disabled individuals who belong in the disabled church. More to the point, until we find ourselves in the disabled church, we will never find the freedom and joy of confessing that we are disabled individuals.

Dietrich Bonhoeffer wrote insightfully about the real character of the Christian family. In *Life Together* he declared,

Dismiss once and for all every clamorous desire for something more. One who wants more than what Christ has established does not want Christian brotherhood. He is looking for some extraordinary social experience which he has not found elsewhere; he is bringing muddled and impure desires into Christian brotherhood. . . . *Christian brotherhood is not an ideal but a divine reality.*

Every human wish dream that is injected into the Christian community is a hindrance to genuine community and must be banished if genuine community is to survive. He who loves his dream of a community more than the Christian community itself is a destroyer of the latter.[4]

In a world that continually tells us to become someone different, better and improved, the church should make the unique claim that it won't help you fulfill such dreams. It can't. It's family.

The church is the place to which we come to be reminded of who we are, not who we want to be. To strive for a dream of the church completely misses the point, just as striving for a dream family does. The tragic result of these dreams is that they turn the church family into yet one more unobtainable demand on our lives.

I've never been too keen on family reunions. I think that's because it's so hard to impress my importance upon the relatives who saw me grow up. They know me too well. At every family gathering with the uncles, aunts and grandparents, it's never long before someone starts telling stories. "Remember when Craig was little and he. . . ."

Like any family, our church is collecting plenty of stories that keep us honest. No function of the church is more important than its role of forcing us to confront the truth about ourselves. By demanding that we live again in a family, the church strips away all pretense. We see ourselves for the broken, needy creatures we've been since the days of our childhood. Then once again, need becomes the altar for worshiping our heavenly Father, who alone is whole and complete.

When we come together, it isn't long before we see the common human realities that lie beneath all appearances. A group of rosy-cheeked young carolers sing joyfully in the home of a shut-in, but they walk away thinking about growing old and lonely. Young mothers meet every Thursday morning, ostensibly for Bible study, but it is never long before they begin to confess their fears about raising children. Two divorced women get together for a quiet dinner to celebrate a birthday. A successful businessman takes a junior-high kid from the housing projects on a fishing trip; they sit in the boat talking about what they have both missed in life.

The fellowship events, the annual traditions, the work camps and the countless potlucks are all ways of creating family memories. These are the vehicles for sharing our stories of loss, loneliness and bad choices.

They create memories of the truth that lies beneath the happy faces and decent lives. When rehearsed later, those memories become the prelude for worship, drawing us to the grace of our Father. Where else would we go once the truth is out?

Are Families in Style Again?

For decades, our society flirted with the illusion that we were individuals who "do our own thing." As adolescents, we thought that if we could leave home we would "find ourselves." Those of us in midlife crisis, disillusioned with how life was turning out, were tempted to believe we could do something dramatic to "find our freedom" from "suffocating commitments." All those trite slogans betray an illusion that life is best understood as an individual freed from the complex, entangling ties of family relationships.

But we're now discovering that we escaped nothing. Psychologists have taught us that though we can leave home, leaving dysfunctional family behavior patterns is another matter. Sociologists tell us that the traditional extended family took a beating over the last thirty years, but the ideal of the family is still very much alive. The Surgeon General tells us that the fear of life-threatening sexually transmitted diseases has made people a little less eager to experiment with extramarital sex. This has all led some to claim that the family is back in style. Even corporations are intent on creating a sense of family, by using management principles that give employees a sense of kinship with their company.

In the midst of this "renewal" of family life, however, we need to be careful to tell the truth about our motivations. We are not returning to the family because we realize that it provides a greater experience than "doing our own thing." We are returning to the family because we realize we're stuck with it. We are stuck with it in our dysfunctional behavior patterns, our fear of AIDS, our recognition of economic interdependence, and our need to work together to resolve the social, political and ecological crises that could kill us all. We have to live together.

About the time that people are again thinking in terms of family, the church has forgotten how to interpret itself as God's family. We are so consumed with preaching the salvation of the individual that we're not ready for those who are asking the church for help in holding relationships together at home and work. Some are doing all they can to make sense of their alcoholic parents, to survive divorce or to cope with children who are substance abusers. Rather than being the prophets and pastors of society, the church has been its competitor, offering a religious version of individualism that heretically claims it is all about you and your self-fulfillment. Even the church's new workshops on divorce, codependency, and the "child within" have frequently been presented with the narcissistic offer of wholeness to the individual. They are seldom concerned about the broken family and its healing.

Yet Scripture is full of stories that indicate how intricately interwoven our lives are. Abraham is called to leave Ur of the Chaldees, but he has commitments and people who love and need him. So he takes along his wife, father and nephew. When his nephew Lot gets in trouble, Abraham is the one who pleads his case with God. The sibling relationships of Cain and Abel, Jacob and Esau, Joseph and his brothers, Moses and Aaron and Miriam, David and his older brothers, James and John, and Peter and Andrew are all rich illustrations of how God finds us as somebody's brother or sister. When the Holy Spirit conceives the hope of the Messiah in the womb of Mary, the life of her fiancé Joseph is dramatically changed. Joseph's experience reminds us that we receive Immanuel, God with us, not only by our own reception of his interruptions but also by the work of God in the lives of those we love. In the church, the interruptions of God change us all by changing some.

This dynamic is marvelously illustrated in Genesis 3. The temptation of Eve immediately becomes the temptation of Adam. Their sin is a communal experience, as are their pain and their experience of God. In sin the created need for intimacy became the anxiety that blamed, divided, and alienated them from each other and the garden they were created to enjoy.

The family can affirm our humanity or corrupt our humanity. But we are never unaffected by family. Even as Adam and Eve leave the garden it is clear that, whatever their future is, it will certainly be a future together.

Family is the place where our past and our future meet to tell us who we are. It is where we find hope. It is what keeps us from finding hope. But clearly, there is no other way.

This is the most important reason we must consider the church to be a family. In the family of God we discover hope and a future, not in spite of our broken relationships but through them. The great difference in the hopeful family of the church and our families of origin is not that the church offers new and improved relationships, this time with our spiritual brothers and sisters. Instead, our hope is found in the gracious love of the new Father, who finds us in the midst of the same dysfunctional relationships at church that we thought we'd left at home.

The Sacrament of Family

Every family has a certain feel to it. Together, the family members of the family add up to more than a mere collection of individuals. In their union, the members create another presence, the personality of the family. This presence is generated by the roles different members play, how they relate to each other, and the mood of the environment that is created when the family is together. Even if the family is apart for years, when it reunites, the same family presence will reappear.

When the church family comes together, it also discovers that its united experience is greater than the sum of the members. Christians believe part of the extra experience that is generated by our gathering is the presence of Christ's own Spirit. "Where two or three come together in my name, there am I with them" (Mt 18:20).

Sometimes the encounter of the presence of God is referred to as the sacramental dimension of the church. Historically, some theologians of the church have stressed its instrumental purpose, while others have emphasized its sacramental experience. But we get the most help from those who speak of the necessity of both.

"Instrumental service" refers to the church's mission to the community. Typically we think of the church's instrumental role as its mission of compassion and charity, the functions it provides for its members, the educational, administrative and pastoral services it offers. Instrumentally, the church is the Spirit's vehicle for moving the future kingdom of God and the present realities closer together.

The "sacramental role" is the experience one has within the functions of the church. If the experience is sacramental, then it is an experience of encountering our God.[5] In the instrumental service, the church functions horizontally, between promise and fulfillment. In the sacramental service it functions vertically, as the place of holy encounter between God and the people he finds.

In the time of the Catholic and Protestant reformations, Reformers such as Luther, Calvin, Erasmus and Loyola all had a place for both dimensions of the church's nature. Over the last several centuries, however, Protestants have usually talked much more about the instrumental function than the sacramental one, while those in the Catholic traditions have frequently done just the opposite. Today we find that the misleading emphasis on one of these purposes at the expense of the other continues to persist.

Some churches call their members simply to participate in the liturgy and receive the sacraments. Yet if liturgical worship is divorced from worship through compassionate service, it is hard to keep our hearts truly open to receiving the God who loves the entire suffering creation. Other churches, typically Protestant, have emphasized the instrumental so much that we've come dangerously close to thinking we can find our own way to God through our slick programs of evangelism, our lay institutes, our mission strategies and our beloved church committees. Our churches are consistently exhorting their members to do, do, do, but are not helping them to receive. I believe Protestants today are hungry for an experience of grace at church. They are missing the sacramental dimension of church life.

Whether a particular Christian tradition celebrates the Lord's Supper weekly is beside the point. At issue is whether our experience of church helps us to stop *doing things* long enough to receive the God who will find us in church—if we let him. That can happen at a Wednesday-night prayer meeting or a Thursday-night choir rehearsal just as easily as it can at Sunday's high mass in a cathedral.

Family Scandals

If the hope of God does find us at church, it is not because we look like the family fathered by God. Having grown up in the church as a pastor's son, I am under no illusions about the moral quality of the church family. I have many memories of how one member hurt another—and how hurtful I was to other kids and to Sunday-school teachers. I certainly remember many painful experiences between the "shepherd" and his "flock." I saw what the church did to my dad, and I saw how Dad hurt the people he thought he loved. I saw the pain at church and the pain in my parents' marriage become so intricately interrelated that the hurting never stopped. Allegations of sexual immorality only added to the complex web of pain. Eventually someone was bound to do something desperate and scandalous. It was the only escape. I used to think that my early church experience was an exception. But since my ordination I have encountered an incredible number of church families in crisis. The church I am currently serving has had a history of ministers in trouble, including one scenario not much different from my parents' experience.

The effects of these experiences are severe. The pain of any member affects the rest of the family, but the desperation and sin of the family's leaders are particularly devastating. It takes a long time for a church to work through the issues of broken trust, anger, and grief.

The amazing quality of the church is not that it fails to live up to its own morality but that it survives its failures. For almost two thousand years this has been our family legacy. We have failed as prophets to society and we failed when we ran society. We've failed in leadership and in charity. But the church was never built upon our performance. The rock of the church has always been the confession of Peter that Jesus is the Christ, the Son of the living God. Whenever the church confesses its sin and failures, it has always been renewed, humbled in recognizing its need for the living God.

Not every church family has to endure the shame of moral failure in its leadership, but all churches are scandalized. This is because all of them live in contradiction to the gospel they preach. It is a scandal that people get mad and leave the family. It is a scandal that people who feel powerless come to the church to be somebody important. It is a scandal that in every church there are those who fill the pews Sunday after Sunday, but who cannot tell the truth about the secret despair that is tearing them apart. Most of all, it's a scandal that God would entrust the proclamation of his grace to a family as dysfunctional as the Christian church. The world is aghast not so much at the church's behavior as at

God's love for the church.

Yet it's in all of this scandal that we find the great secret of the gospel. And the secret is this: it is not until we confess how scandalously inadequate we are even to talk about grace that we are finally ready to receive it.

The church that my parents abandoned has recovered from its days of grief. It continues to try to live by the same grace Dad once proclaimed there. In the church I now serve, the husband of the wife who left with one of the pastors still attends worship regularly. When I see him in the congregation I become filled with hope—hope that my parishioners know what it means to find God in the midst of their brokenness. This man's son is a pastor, serving a church ten miles away from ours. We frequently get together to talk about the families we love. We talk about our parents, and about how our wounds have become places for spirituality and ministry to grow. Of course, we also talk a lot about our church families.

We pray together for our churches, asking that we will not hurt them. I doubt we will repeat the sins of our parents, but ours is a futile prayer all the same. We are bound to hurt our congregations somehow. After all, we're family.

The Holy Family

Any claim that at church we encounter the gracious presence of God is rightly countered with a pressing question. How can we encounter God when the church family is so dysfunctional and even sinful?

Actually, this is a pretty old question. In many of Paul's epistles there are evidences of the early church's struggle with it. But the question seems to have reached its full force in the Donatist controversy, in the fourth century. After Christianity was legalized with the conversion of Emperor Constantine, the church entered a period of great uncertainty about its identity. Born out of persecution, the church had spent its first three centuries as a body of extremely committed members, willing to follow Christ to their deaths. After it became legal, however, it was transformed from a body of persecuted subversives into the most favored religion of the empire and eventually the state religion. In 311, a bishop named Felix consecrated Caecilian as bishop of Carthage. Trouble arose because Felix had been a traitor to the church during the severe persecutions that had immediately preceded Constantine's conversion. Many felt the ordination of Caecilian was not valid, because it had been conducted by Felix. Some split from the church and set up the rival bishop Majorinus, who was soon followed by Donatus. The church of Donatus grew strong until, by 350, it was the dominant church in North Africa.

Purity was the theological hallmark of the Donatists. The symbol of the church they embraced was not the cross but the ark—the vessel that had kept the pure safe from the judgment of God upon the world. Ordination by one who was not pure meant that guilt, not purity, was passed on. Thus, for the Donatists, guilt was received by association. The holiness of the church was determined, then, by the holiness of its members. Donatists rebaptized converts from the Roman church, because no one outside of their own pure church was considered Christian.

This separated church continued until 412, when it was condemned by St. Augustine. His refutation of the Donatists centered on three claims.

First, he stated that dividing the church is itself a sin, and so the purity of any separated body is a contradiction. Second, Scripture makes it quite clear that the wheat and the tares of the church are to grow together until God separates them. Augustine was under no illusions that everyone in the Christian society was a Christian, but he was also clear about the limitations of the church in setting standards of holiness. Third, and most significant, he reminded the Donatists that the holiness of the church resides in the head and not the members of Christ's body. This holiness is found, he claimed, in the holy sacraments, the holy Scriptures, and the holy doctrine of the church, all of which bring us to Christ, the church's head. For Augustine, the church was a holy means of grace, but not necessarily a collection of holy people.

This has great implications for the contemporary church. Many of us are knocking ourselves out to define the church by its boundaries. These boundaries make it clearly evident who is in the church and who is out. We want everyone in the church to look, talk and think like the head of the church. What Augustine (and a subsequent string of theologians including Luther and Calvin) claimed was that the church is defined by its center and not its boundaries.

At the center of the church we find the holiness of Christ proclaimed in Word and sacrament. That means that the church may contain all sorts of people who look, talk and think as if they didn't belong there—which, of course, is exactly why they *do* belong there.

No one deserves to be a family member. We receive that identity not by rights but by grace. We did not choose the families in which we grew up. In fact, we were born or adopted into families made up of individuals we might not have chosen if we had met them as adults. But that's beside the point. It doesn't matter whether we like them—they're family. We can't choose to leave the family and dissociate ourselves from that identity. No matter how hard one tries to disinherit a family member, history cannot be changed. The family we grew up in is the family we're stuck with.

All this holds true for the church as well. We are part of the church, not because we deserve to be there, not even because we want to be there, but because being there is critical to our identity. There is no other way for us to know who we are in the faith.

The parish I serve is an easy church to join. We work hard at making it easy for people to get in. If they will confess that Jesus Christ is their Lord and Savior, and if they vow to make diligent use of the means of grace through hearing the Word proclaimed, receiving the sacraments and participating in the church's community, then we make them part of the family.

Beyond that common confession, we couldn't write a church doctrinal statement if our lives depended on it. We don't agree on what it means to call Christ Lord in light of our politics, our finances or even our theology. Some in the church are liberal and some are conservative. Some are conservative theologically and liberal politically. Others, it seems, are liberal theologically and quite conservative politically. Some are intensely loyal to our denomination, and others don't trust it for a minute. Some come to church with well-worn study Bibles, and others couldn't find Genesis if it weren't for the index. Some members like the pastors and other church leaders, and some don't. In fact, the only thing that holds our family together is the one head of the household—the God we know in Jesus Christ.

As in any family, we even have different relationships with our Father. But we are all in the family because we received the Father when he came looking for us. For that reason alone, our family is holy, even though we sure don't look like it by many definitions.

We have discovered two wonderful effects of this philosophy of church membership. First, besides the fact that it makes our committee meetings very interesting, it provides repeated reminders that our only hope for being a church family is in the one Father. Every deadlocked decision forces us to prayer. We don't move ahead as quickly as churches with less diversity, but we do frequently move back to God.

Second, we have discovered that a diverse church has a valuable witness to the diverse families of the world. People are looking for a place to belong without the tyranny of conformity. Our mission to the complex world around us has much more hope when the church gives up trying to re-create people into what we imagine "Christians" should look like. Our family needs newly adopted brothers and sisters who enrich our life together by bringing their unique experience of the gospel. This is the difference between unity and cultic sameness. In seeking unity, the church is held together only by its common Lord, never by the uniformity of its members.

Diversity in the church also confronts us with the ever-present reminder that any one of us could be wrong in our interpretation of God's Word. Again, that humbles and brings us back to the only thing about which we are all certain—we live by grace.

Summery and Wintry Christians

Not all family members feel at home in the house of God. This is not just because they find the traditions and language of a particular church strange or foreign. More profoundly, they may consider the church traditions strange because they are not at all sure about the presence of the Father of the family. Yet they are family members nonetheless. Perhaps their faith in the promise of the Father's presence is so great that they have taken seriously the apparent contradictions of reality. But their struggle over the "lost" Father makes them uncomfortable if the family traditions include only songs, prayers and testimonials that focus on his obvious presence.

The late Catholic theologian Karl Rahner taught that the church must always make room for two different types of spirituality. He referred to these in their extreme forms as "Summery" and "Wintry."[6]

Summery Christians have a "hot" faith. They are known for their unquestioning belief in the presence of God. They can see him at work.

Theirs is a God who answers when called, who talks to his children in prayer and who provides clear signs of his caring compassion. Summery faith is expressed in "Praise the Lord!" These people's spirituality is so warm, however, that it tends to alienate Wintry brothers and sisters, who find that their faith cannot survive in such heat.

The Wintry Christian believes God should be present but in all honesty is more acutely aware of God's absence. These Christians are drawn to the psalms of lament and to the New Testament images of knocking and seeking. They understand that God is as compassionate as the Summery Christians profess him to be, but they are bothered by all the unrelieved pain and loneliness of the Father's children.

The Wintry Christian searches for a God of grace, while the Summery revels in a God of glory. Wintry Christians tend to ignore passages that affirm the joy of our salvation, while Summery Christians tend to ignore the realities of starving children, death squads and economic injustice. Wintry Christians are always looking for meaning, and Summery Christians are always looking for mission. Summery types are constantly asking God to show them where they should go; Wintry Christians would love to tell Summery Christians where to go, but the two types rarely talk to each other. The Wintry faith is a lonely, soul-searching spirituality, while Summery faith is best practiced with other Summery Christians.

Both of these, Rahner cautions, are authentic expressions of the faith. Both have strong biblical grounding and clear theological foundations. Neither should be excluded from the church, nor should either be granted a monopoly. Both need the family, but for different reasons. The Wintry sort need their brothers and sisters to walk beside them through their lonely doubts and struggles. The Summery Christians need the family to provide consistent affirmations of the faith as a way of rehearsing their identity. The worst thing we can do is to expect one to act like the other. The church needs both. Where would we be without the changing seasons of summer and winter? They are both part of God's cycle.

Traditionally, the American Protestant church has been very accepting of Summery Christians, because their enthusiasm blends well with the American spirit. It is critical, though, that we not absolutize this one expression of family life, as if God had favorite children. As Martin Marty has claimed, we do that whenever we insist that the family of God can live only in our particular tribal hut.[7]

As the Wintry Christians make their way through the lonely woods of doubt, confusion and disorienting loss, they look, maybe even longingly, at the great variety of huts all claiming to be warmed by God's presence.[8] There is the light and airy family hut of the liberals. Here are lofty views but no real foundations. There is the long hut of the fundamentalist family, solidly constructed of packed mud, but so thick that no one can see out of it. The electronic-ministry huts are elegant and vividly decorated, but their inhabitants seem preoccupied with their own hut's maintenance. Spiritual best sellers emerge from some huts with the promise that if we'll just follow their prescriptions and think right thoughts, all of the chill will disappear for our Wintry siblings. Still others leave their huts long enough to pull a sacred canopy over all of society so none of the acid rain of secularity will be felt on their public schools, legislatures or media.

The problem for the Wintry Christian is that by definition a family hut is meant to keep the cold out and the warmth in. Wintry Christians need a brother or sister to walk through the cold with them, but will always resist invitations to settle into a cozy hut. Churches will often find that Wintry types stay just long enough to get warmed up and then, if the church cannot tolerate their challenging doubts or cold skepticism, leave as quickly as they arrived.

Frankly, Wintry Christians can drive you nuts just as fast the Summery variety. But our family can never exclude the troubled brothers and sisters who keep asking those hard questions about our absentee Father. The church must hear the quiet cries of those who, in spite of having the right theology, still feel lost in the midst of so many who claim to be saved. Their Wintry journey is tiring, and the family needs to give them rest, not interrogation, when they finally make it home.

The Family in the World

When the holy family of the church presents itself to the other families of the earth in its true character as a diverse, compromised, needy and certainly broken family, it is then best prepared to assume its evangelistic function.

The world around us is not impressed by the church's efforts to market itself as a group of people who are somehow better than the rest of the world. What does impress the world is the truth—the truth about how painful life is and the truth about our inescapable need for grace if we are to survive. The content of the church's witness is to invite others to join in the fellowship of the suffering, where we come together to discover the only hope we've got (Phil 3:10).

I believe people are desperately searching for such a distinctive family. Most of the other families to which they've belonged have made promises, common dreams and even pretense the criteria for admittance. Never confession. It is such a relief to enter a place where others are boldly claiming that they are never going to be whole and complete, no matter how hard they try. But of course, that's only half of the gospel. The other half of the good news is that needs and limitations are the best opportunity we have to receive God's grace. And God's grace is what we were created to enjoy together from the beginning.

Accordingly, evangelism is best understood as a function of the family, not the individual. It's the church that is Christ's true witness, not the soul-winner who attempts to go it alone. Just as we can never understand individuals apart from their families, we can never understand the Christian apart from the church. Neither can we understand the church apart from the world in which it is called to exist, and which it often resembles.

Granted, when you are trying to impress someone it can be embarrassing to bring him or her to your home. Some fear that when non-Christians see our church family, they may have good reason to question the effectiveness of our hope. But to try to convince someone of the value of God's grace based on any rationale other than human need is to misconstrue both our nature and the nature of grace. When we evangelize by avoiding our dysfunctional family, we are lying. We then become dishonest door-to-door salespeople rather than confessors of a real family's hope. When we witness by allowing the church to live in the world with its message of grace, we take on the world's brokenness and become the broken but hopeful family of God.

———

SO THE LORD GOD BANISHED [ADAM] FROM THE GARDEN

OF EDEN TO WORK THE GROUND FROM

WHICH HE HAD BEEN TAKEN. AFTER HE DROVE THE MAN

OUT, HE PLACED ON THE EAST SIDE OF THE

GARDEN OF EDEN CHERUBIM AND A FLAMING SWORD

FLASHING BACK AND FORTH TO GUARD THE

WAY TO THE TREE OF LIFE.

GENESIS 3 : 2 3 - 2 4

SLOW KINGDOM COMING

8

There is no real hope for the individual or the church if there is not also hope for the world in which we live. The path to hope for the world is the same path the individual and the church must follow. It is the path into brokenness, where we discover that we and the hurting world are found by our God.

The world's condition is severe. It is the brokenness of humanity written large. We cannot be genuinely involved in it and maintain our illusions about wholeness.

Displacement

A few professionally successful persons from our church decided to go to the soup kitchen to help out. When they arrived one night, they discovered they were not going to just dish out the slop to the bums. Instead, the director of the kitchen invited them to sit across the table from those who were the guests that night. After a few clumsy moments, a conversation began. Soon they were listening to stories they will never forget.

Turns out one "bum" is the young mother of four children. If you look hard, you can still see the traces of beauty fading from her rough, weathered face. She didn't plan on being hungry and homeless, or on raising her children in an unending series of shelters, motels and borrowed cars. In better days, she was somebody's date to the prom, the quiet girl who lived down the street, and even the pretty bride who marched down the aisle confident that she had the world by the tail. But physical abuse, or drug abuse, or just the abuse of a hard world put an end to those days. Now she is lost.

Our middle-class do-gooders drove home that night asking questions that don't have easy answers. "How did this happen to her? What's to keep that from happening to me? Why didn't God intervene?" These questions came back to mind the next Sunday morning when everybody stood in church to sing, "Praise God from whom all blessings flow."

What happened that night at the soup kitchen? Having taken the time to see the world for the hard place it is, Christians were displaced from the secure place they'd found for themselves. There was more to the world than they'd thought. They'd always been vaguely aware of poverty as an issue, but now that issue had faces and names, and stories that could not be forgotten. Now, to sing the doxology required a greater knowledge of God than they had previously cherished. What does it say about God that so many have received so few of the flowing blessings?

Whenever the church looks at the world in which it dwells, it is forced to see the world's pain. Responding to that pain will have dramatic implications for what goes on in the pulpit and the pew. Missions is critical to the spiritual vitality of the church, not because we ought to go into the world, but because through engaging the world each of us is disabused of the illusion that the gospel is all about me. In missions we discover the hard truth that we were not so fortunate, just insulated. Now we have to discover a God with longer arms than we'd previously imagined, arms embracing those without many visible blessings. That is one of the graces of living in a harsh world.

This is not just a theological problem. Christians who regularly confront the harder side of the world have to confront their own insecurity. Now it is more difficult to separate our fate from that of the world around us. Now we realize how fragile our private and church "worlds" are as well. We aren't really separated from the perils and problems of the wider world. Whatever God does for his world, and what he does for us, has to become part of the same story.

Living toward a Vision: "The Healing of the Nations"

The end of our story from Genesis 3 makes it clear that we are all a long, long way from the serenity of our home in the garden. But, of course, that's not the end of the biblical story. The end of that bigger story looks like this:

> Then the angel showed me the river of the water of life, as clear as crystal, flowing from the throne of God and of the Lamb down the middle of the great street of the city. On each side of the river stood the tree of life, bearing twelve crops of fruit, yielding its fruit every month. And the leaves of the tree are for the healing of the nations. (Rev 22:1-2)

For almost two thousand years Christians have been inspired and comforted by the vision of Revelation. We may argue with each other about the timing and schemes for how this City of God will be built, but we are united in our belief that God has a hopeful future for the world that he loves. Somewhere, somehow, there is another tree in our future—the tree of life.

Our souls long for the fruit of that tree. We may not be able to make our way back to paradise, but Scripture clearly offers a vision for the place of the tree of life in our future. The nations will find their healing from its branches. This great vision reassures us that God has not abandoned us to our present crises. Just as the fruit of one tree symbolized our great Fall, so the fruit of the tree of life represents our longing to live eternally. The world is hungry for a future.

The important question is, How does this vision help us to live in the meantime—caught between how it is and how it will be? That is what all the chapters between Genesis 3 and Revelation 22 are about. These chapters, the body of the Bible, claim that it's up to God to give his world a future. All we can do is receive it as it arrives.

This truth affects the shape of Christian mission. If nothing else, it certainly follows that we stand with a vision not just for our own healing but also for the healing of the nations of the world. Actually, we don't stand as much as we kneel. The better we get at confessing our world's needs and brokenness, the more hope we have of receiving the healing that only God can offer.

The Kingdom Coming

Everything that the Bible says about the future is meant to help us live better in the present. Scripture speaks about this future as the coming kingdom, the long-awaited ordering of all human life according to the purposes and will of God. We are promised that this visible reign of God is on the way. But this promise was never meant to be a comforting reassurance that someday things will get better if we just believe. Rather, Scripture uses kingdom-of-God language consistently as a way of speaking about the present.

The coming kingdom *of God* stands in contrast to all the kingdoms of this world. Our citizenship in God's kingdom prevents us from having other gods, including any nationalistic pride that comes at the expense of God's people outside our nation. When nationalism steps over that line, it has ceased to be a mark of good citizenship and has become instead a blatant idolatry. God's kingdom is never, never limited to the borders of a nation. Yet all nations—Christian, Jewish and Muslim—are tempted to limit God's kingdom to their own. Because we all feel our vulnerability and needs acutely, we try to wrap geographic borders around the chosen people of God.

Never has our nation struggled with this conflict between God's kingdom and our own quite as it did during the Civil War. Both Northern and Southern pastors assured their congregations that God was on their side, that the battle into which their men were heading was a holy one. With great wisdom and humility, President Lincoln cautioned the churches against saying God is on our side. Instead, he called them to pray that we all be on the side of God, whose ways transcend our own. He expressed this call most eloquently in his second inaugural address:

Both [the North and the South] read the same Bible, and pray to the same God and each invokes his aid against the other. It may seem strange that any men should dare to ask a just God's assistance in wringing their bread from the sweat of other men's faces; but let us not judge that we be not judged. The prayers of both could not be answered; and that of neither has been answered fully. The Almighty has his own purposes. . . . Fondly do we hope—fervently do we pray—that this mighty scourge of war may soon pass away. . . .

With malice toward none; with charity for all; with firmness in the right as God gives us to see the right, let us strive on to finish the work we are in; to bind up the nation's wounds; to care for him who shall have borne the battle, and for his widow and his orphan—to do all which may achieve and cherish a just and lasting peace among ourselves and with all nations.[1]

Lincoln, the son of a devout Baptist, never lost the conviction that while we may be the instruments of "the Almighty," he is certainly never the instrument of any one of our divided kingdoms.

Second, to affirm our allegiance to the coming *kingdom* of God means that the church strives to bring all of life under God's reign. We cannot confess our needs and vulnerability in church while living by the power agendas of the world from Monday to Saturday. If the church has discovered that need is a created condition, given to bind us to our Creator, then we have to live by that truth every day of the week. One of the church's great responsibilities is to help its members learn how to live in the world that has become alien to them. This doesn't mean that we turn our back on the world or ignore its impassioned pleas for deliverance, but it does mean that Christians must never forget how to live in the world as citizens of the new kingdom. We remain very involved in the world but cannot feel at home with its ethics.

Third, to believe in the *coming* kingdom of God means that we live as if the present were open. There is more to this day than we may see. There is also hope, and that is not necessarily good news. As Walter Brueggemann has said, "Hope reminds us that the way things are is precarious and in jeopardy. Hope reminds us not to absolutize the present, not to take it too seriously, not to treat it too honorably, because it will not last."[2]

Our hope as Christians is not that someday things will get better for us. Actually, our ship may never come in. A cure for the disease may not be found in time, the perfect woman could have married someone else by now, and things may not go well after we've moved to the next town. Nor is it our hope that the good things in life will last eternally.

Stock markets can crash, health can fade, and relationships can certainly take a turn for the worse. It is as wrong for us to wait for life to begin in the future as it is to assume that the life we now have will never change.

Our hope is that God is building his kingdom today. That may involve as many losses as gains for most of us. Our hope may involve the future, but it does not rest there, any more than it does in fiercely holding onto what we have today. Christian hope certainly means that if we are counting on anything other than the work of God, sooner or later we'll lose it. Because the promise is clear: his kingdom is coming.

Caught between Good Friday and Easter

When the kingdom finally comes, it will come as a complete surprise. Jesus made this fact perfectly clear. In Scripture we're told quite a bit about God's coming Kingdom, but never when it will fully arrive. Some passages indicate that it will come soon. Others make the point that no one knows when it will come. We've learned that it certainly comes later than we'd expected. In the meantime, while we wait, we live as if we were already citizens of the kingdom. We adopt its values. We work hard for its fulfillment as if its coming depended on us (though of course it does not). Some would argue that in the church's proclamation the kingdom is already present. But that does little to soothe the anxiety of those who are afraid to pick up newspapers every morning.

God is not bound by our expectations—not even by our expectations of his own promises. The people of faith spend most of their lives caught somewhere between promise and fulfillment. Significantly, it is in this hard place that faith gains its meaning. There would be no need for faith if God came through every time we knocked on his door. Yet to believe the promise in the face of contradictory realities is what God's people have always done best. That means the church lives and works in the world guided by the truth of the vision for a kingdom that God has given us, even if that timeless truth seems challenged by the shifting sands of today's reality.

I've always thought the day after the crucifixion must have been the worst day in history. The disciples had just witnessed the death of all their hopes on the cross of Jesus Christ. They knew that he was really dead. Not pretend dead, not almost dead but soon to recover—completely dead. Although Jesus had made allusions to his rising from the dead, it is clear that not a one of them had any clue what that was all about. With the passing of Friday, all hope was completely lost. When Easter came, it took everyone completely by surprise.

Most churches today couldn't get a crowd up for Good Friday Services if their life depended on it. In our town many churches cooperate in a joint service, and we still can't get a half-filled sanctuary. But on Easter, we always have to set up extra chairs at the extra services we plan.

Why is that? Is it because hope sells better than despair? If that is true, then most of our people are missing the real place of hope. We don't find authentic hope by rushing to Easter joy. Rather, hope is found in the time between Good Friday and Easter—or Just Plain Saturday. All of creation finds itself there, as we continue to wait between the death of our expectations of what God would do and the fulfillment of his true promises.

Luke 18:1-8 records a significant parable Jesus told his disciples. An elderly widow of little importance makes her way into the busy chambers of a judge to ask for justice. Although her welfare is the judge's responsibility, he has little time for her and sends her away. But all she has is her persistence, so she just keeps coming to the judge, demanding that he give her justice.

She finally wears him down, and he gives her what she wants. When Jesus gets to the moral of the story, he says, "Listen to what the unjust judge says. And will not God bring about justice for his chosen ones, who cry out to him day and night? Will he keep putting them off? I tell you, he will see that they get justice, and quickly. However, when the Son of Man comes, will he find faith on the earth?"

I don't think Jesus gave us this parable to tell us that persistence in prayer will eventually pay off. As anyone knows who has tried it enough, prayer doesn't always bring the answer we want. Perhaps the deeper point lies in the relationship of the promise that is made to the question that is asked. The promise is that it is God who will bring about the kingdom of justice. And the crucial question is, "Will there be any faith left on earth when it finally gets here?" For the early-church readers of Luke's Gospel, the parable was meant to encourage them to keep believing in the kingdom, to hope and work for it and to cry out to God for it—like a helpless old widow.

If Faith Is to Persevere . . .

Although the world is still in sorry shape in spite of all the church's proclamation of the kingdom, we have learned some things over the centuries. We have learned that the faith of some in the kingdom perseveres while others' faith does not. A faith that always perseveres always tells the truth. To avoid the truth is not faith—it is fantasy, and fantasy never lasts. Faith is born out of wrestling with the truth, and the truth of the matter is that the kingdom hasn't come. Not yet.

It is fantasy to think that the world can literally go to hell since I have my salvation, since the judge has taken care of me. Not only is it a fantasy, but it is a dangerous fantasy, because my salvation is integrally tied up with God's love for the world. In the words of Karl Barth,

When we convert and are renewed in the totality of our being, we cross the threshold of our private existence and move out into the open. The inner problems may be most urgent and burning and exciting, but we are not engaged in conversion if we confine our-selves to them. We simply run (in a rather more subtle way) on our own path headlong into destruction. When we convert and are re-newed in the totality of our being, in and with our private respon-sibility we also accept a public responsibility. For it is the great God of heaven and earth who is for us, and we are for this God.[3]

The credibility of the kingdom is on the line every time we see pictures of hungry children and other signs of the oppression that keeps abound-ing despite our repeated pleas for justice. To believe in a God who says he loves the world is to stand in the chasm between the promise of how it should be and the reality of how it is.

As Barth also taught us, this means we must hold our newspaper in one hand and our Bible in the other. We carry in the one hand our public responsibility and in the other hand our theological commit-ments. Each demands the other, but it is very difficult to hold them together. You see, there is no safe side to belief. God has not made his world whole, any more than he has made that fantasy come true for the individual. If faith is to persevere, it has to account for the delay in God's "healing of the nations."

On October 17, 1989, people all over the United States rushed to their TV screens to find out about the terrible earthquake in San Francisco. During one of the video clips I noticed something that was lying on the ground behind a reporter. Against the rubble of a fallen building there was an open umbrella. It was tattered and broken, but it was definitely an umbrella. In the midst of all the destruction no one seemed to notice it, but I became fascinated with how it got there. Maybe, I thought, somebody had left for work that day with no worries other than whether it would rain.

Then it occurred to me that it wasn't raining when the earthquake hit—but the umbrella was open. "Could it be," I thought, "that with buildings, expressways and bridges falling down, someone tried to find protection by opening a nylon umbrella?"

Sometimes, when the world shakes around us, life is so frightening that we'll do anything to give ourselves the illusion of security. We'll hide under the thin canopy of our personal faith, hoping that God will at least protect us as the world begins to crumble.

But any church that takes seriously its call to be a church in the world soon finds that it cannot hide, certainly not under the thin umbrella of private faith. When faith becomes a guide to the church's journey in the world, rather than an umbrella, realistic hope can emerge. That faith will take us on a journey that is not easy, because it forces us to struggle not only with the conditions of our world but also with the nature of our God who is so slow in healing it. As Simone Weil has written,

> One can never wrestle enough with God if one does so out of pure regard for the truth. In fact, Christ invites us to prefer truth even to him. Because before being the Christ, he is the truth. If one turns aside from him to go toward the truth, one will not go far before falling into his arms.[4]

Faith is a huge risk for all Christians who tell the truth. The risk is not that their beliefs in the compassion of God will be proved wrong. Not really. The far greater risk is that their faith will lead them to discover more of the truth than they want to know. On this journey Christians will certainly be led to a place they would rather not go—maybe even back to the world.

The Second Conversion

It is easy for us to become so elated at the alternative Christ offers us that we see the world as the church's enemy rather than the object of its compassion. But for a Christian to walk away from the world is to begin a journey in the wrong direction. This is certainly not a journey toward God. We might say that Christians require a second conversion. In this second conversion, the heart repents of its resentment toward the world, and we turn back to the place from which we first came. But now we journey into the world with God, and with new eyes and hearts. Now our eyes are searching for Christ's involvement, and our hearts, rather than being tortured by fear and insecurity, are filled with compassion.

It seems to me that this pivotal change comes when we discover some sense of Christ's kingdom at work in the world. We begin to understand that God is found better in mission to the world than through calls to purity and separation. But this second conversion cannot take place until we see God in the places we've been running from.

In his great novel *The Brothers Karamazov,* Fyodor Dostoyevsky portrays this journey in the character of Alexei Karamazov. Having discovered that the world is too harsh and dark, Alexei retreats to a monastery in hope of finding some light and beauty. While he is there, his best friend and mentor dies. The mentor's dying wish is that Alexei learn to live in the world. On the night the old man dies, Alexei has a dream in which he comes upon the wedding at Cana and finds his mentor drinking wine with Jesus. At first Alexei is terrified at being in the presence of the Christ, but his friend tells him,

> Don't be frightened of him. Though he is frightening in his greatness, terrifying in his majesty, he is also infinitely merciful, and out of love has made himself like one of us . . . and shares our joy, and turns our water into wine, so that the joy of the guests shall not cease, and he invites more and more guests, unceasingly, more new guests forever and ever.[5]

Having been in the presence of God, Alexei is able to leave the monastery. He walks out the door, falls on the ground and hugs it, watering the earth with tears of joy and love. At last he is able to embrace the harsh world. Why? Because he has seen God. And he has seen him not as a vengeful God of judgment but as the God who delights in the people he created and shares in their joy.

We are so certain of God's anger and judgment, but so unsure of his mercy and compassion. At first it is almost offensive to us that God would be found in what we consider the "wrong" places. But if we look carefully, there's no mistaking that it is God we see at the wedding, at the office, at the food bank, in the shelter and in the public schools. Why is he there? Out of love he has "made himself like one of us."

As long as God can be seen, we have every reason in the world to be joyful and to live passionately in all the common places. It is as if we were born again—again.

Looking for the Kingdom

So the great task for the faithful is to pray for the vision to see God at work in the world, and then to wholeheartedly embrace the glimpse we get of his glorious future. The Christian journey is frequently punctuated with transforming moments that give us this glimpse of God in the world.

That is one of the enduring messages of the postresurrection narratives of Scripture. After Jesus' death, Mary goes in search of him on Sunday morning. Not finding him in the grave where he is supposed to be, she becomes frantic. She comes across a man she thinks is the cemetery gardener. Taking her anger and pain out on him, she demands, "Where is he? Where is the dead Savior?" Not until the risen Jesus calls her name does she discover who the "gardener" is. In that moment the common and the ordinary become the vessel of the sacred, and Mary receives the frightening, unimaginable truth. Her Hope could not remain dead. She has not been abandoned at all; it is only that she could not see the Christ who was with her. Who would have thought?

It was the gardener all along.

Most Christians do not enjoy extraordinary encounters with God. This is not to debunk the stories of those who've had supernatural experiences. God is God and can reveal himself however he wants.

But most of us are found by God in quieter transforming moments, not all that different from Mary's experience. In such moments the ordinary events of life suddenly take on new meaning. God may use any event to leave you with an enduring conviction about his kingdom. It doesn't have to be dramatic—usually these events aren't.

You are vacuuming in the living room. You look out the window and notice your son playing with one of his friends. It occurs to you for the first time that someday he is going to leave home, and you are going to miss him. You start to live with a deeper conviction about taking seriously the few fleeting years you'll have with him.

At an office meeting, your mind drifts away from the presentation. You look across the table into the faces of people with whom you have worked for years. It suddenly occurs to you that you know nothing about these people, and yet you spend more time with them than your own family. You leave the meeting wondering how to care for these whom you've been unable to see, though they are so close.

Exhausted after a long day, you step into the elevator of a busy building. As it makes its way down, you get the feeling someone is staring at you. You look up and notice that the someone is a Down's syndrome child. He smiles a kind of goofy smile and says "Hi!" You gently smile back, but inside your heart has melted. Years of social conditioning prevent you from hugging him and saying that he's just made your day. But you step off the elevator with another chip of your stony exterior chiseled away; a bit more of the kingdom has entered your life.

These are all life-transforming moments—common events inflamed with eternal significance. The question isn't whether or not God speaks to us. When scriptural truth is applied to our common routines, we find God speaking to us all the time—usually through the gardener. The real question is, Are we listening? Are we willing to receive the kingdom as it slowly changes our lives and our perceptions of the needy world around us?

Two of Jesus' followers, Cleopas and another, were quietly making their way down the road to Emmaus after their Lord was crucified. The risen Christ began to walk with them, but, typically, they did not recognize him. Along the way they spoke of their despair. Eventually the disciples invited this man to join them for dinner. "So he went in to stay with them. When he was at the table with them, he took bread, gave thanks, broke it and began to give it to them. Then their eyes were opened and they recognized him, and he disappeared from their sight" (Lk 24:29-31).

I love this part of the story. The image of the Risen Lord holding the broken bread eternally signifies God holding our broken dreams and broken bodies, our broken homes and broken fellowships, and our sophisticated world that has broken down under the weight of its sin— and all of it has been cradled in his own brokenness. In that communion the disciples' eyes are opened, and in that moment Jesus vanishes.

If we can find Christ in no other transforming moment, we certainly can see him in the Holy Supper that he instituted for the church. The sacrament of Communion always invites us to a shift in our perceptions. As we approach the table with the Lord, we move from the unrecognized visible presence to the recognized invisible presence. The common bread and plain old wine are visibly present, but unrecognized as the body and blood of Christ. But as the sacrament of grace, those elements give way to a recognition of the Christ who is with us.

As quickly as he comes, he disappears. Just as Christ is not contained by the bread and the wine, he is not contained by our dreams. He will vanish every time we try to grab him and cram him into our expectations. But we know that it was Jesus who broke into our brokenness. We don't know what it means. We don't know where it will lead, but we know he was here. He is here.

Since we have seen the God of eternity, the present is no longer the same. Having seen that God, we have to turn our attention back to the world. That is where he found us, and that is where he leads us.

Christian Mission to a Broken World

Our mission to the world cannot make creation whole again, any more than we can create wholeness in ourselves or our churches. We offer the world only the grace of God, and that can never be confused with problem solving. It is high time we let go of all mission strategies that offer optimistic social agendas for the world. Instead, our mission is to live in the midst of brokenness that we cannot fix with a vision of God's healing—healing from the damage people have wrought by playing God in the world.

Christians do not fulfill this vision by grand schemes that re-create the world, but by their faithfulness in going into all the world as the Christian community of hope. Thus the church does not address the world with its mission agenda as much as it opens the doors of its community to include the world.

When the apostles left Jerusalem to fulfill their great commission, they did not immediately lobby Rome for a better social policy, nor did they invest their mission dollars in a task force that would write position papers or call for candlelight vigils on the steps of Caesar's home. What they did was plant communities of hope wherever they could.

Granted, these hopeful churches were in fact subversive to the oppressive political order, but only because they were effective in transforming the part of the world in which they lived. Early Christians took abandoned babies into their homes, took care of the aged and the widowed, modeled compassion in their relationships with each other, offered a vision of history that gave meaning and order in volatile times, and provided a place where slave and free were both respected.

Seldom has the world found hope when Christians have adopted its strategies for effecting change. That effort has only baptized power models that the world has already found ineffective. Worse, this approach betrays the integrity of our gospel. We make this mistake when we rush to legitimate the nation's battles as holy wars, and we make it when we allow the church to become the puppet of those whose ideology is rooted in resisting their government. In either case, the church is cramming its theology into the secular language of politicians and sociologists. We make the same mistake when we spend all our mission dollars on Washington lobbyists and denominational task forces that produce theologically empty and politically naive position papers. Sooner or later it all comes down to the church's fascination with the world's power politics.

Our understanding of change, of redemption, is permanently rooted in the powerlessness of the cross. We cannot hope to witness to the strange power of God by adopting the addictive, power-hungry agendas of those God seeks to redeem.

By contrast, the world has always discovered hope when Christians have stood in the midst of a dark reality with a vision they cherished enough to suffer for—whether in the arenas of Rome or the streets of Birmingham. In the words of a seminary professor I know, "Don't just do something. Stand there." Stand in the places of injustice and oppression, and stand in the places of power and wealth. Stand beside the good and the evil. Stand with the sick and dying in Calcutta, and with the sick and dying in the singles bars of New York. Stand in the world as a missionary of God's reconciliation, who does not want to give the world what it asks nearly as much as he wants to give himself.

Does this rigid commitment to the gospel mean that Christians must content themselves with offering the world apocalyptic schemes while injustice and oppression continue to abound? Of course not. It does mean that the church has no social or political program for the world. But it also means that the gospel we speak to the world must be accompanied by our hard work to bring God's healing to those who have been broken and hurt.

A couple of years ago our church became committed to helping kids whom the public schools had labeled "at risk" of dropping out. At first we began to work with Young Life to provide weekly tutoring for some of these students. But we soon began to realize that the challenges these kids faced went far beyond getting through the next algebra exam. There were challenges at home as well as in the school system. There were great challenges in the city of Madison, which is often so impressed with its progressive image that it cannot admit its ghettoizing of minorities. Wanting to do more for the kids, we were tempted to attack the problem. Before we knew it, we were on a crusade to fix things. With a vengeance we began to look at all the agencies and political and educational systems that needed to be lobbied and manipulated to meet our desired goals. After all, isn't that the way the world works?

When we heard ourselves asking that question, we knew we were in trouble. So we began to ask better questions, such as, What is the church uniquely qualified to do here? How has life in God's kingdom equipped us to respond to this great need in our city?

It wasn't long before we stopped acting like angry lobbyists and began instead to work toward bringing these kids and their families into our understanding of a loving community. That doesn't mean we made them Presbyterians. We didn't. What we did was introduce them to life in the kingdom—we started working harder on relationships and less on realizing our naive hopes of alleviating poverty and racism in all of Madison. The kids and their families then became not "the problem" but the valuable people we wanted to love.

We also expanded our relationships with community organizations who shared our concern. We became partners not only with Young Life but also with our local community foundation and several business leaders. Soon "Project Opportunity" was launched, with the focus of providing opportunity for sixteen "at risk" kids and their families. The Madison Community Foundation allocated grant money to run the program and pay a full-time director. We provided funds from our church endowment to send the kids to college if they graduate from high school. And far more important, we provided some of the mentors. Soon we realized that we couldn't limit the opportunity to only sixteen families. Quickly another fifty relationships were made around the same model, with other churches coming on board to work in a common ministry of relationships.

We realized that it would be best if the black kids had black mentors, which prompted us to seek the Union Tabernacle Church of God in Christ. Its members were eager to work with most of the black students and to provide healthy role models to encourage the kids to break out of a degrading system of dependency.

Then we discovered a gift no one had expected—the partners began to trust each other.

The Madison Community Foundation, which took leadership for the program, discovered that churches are the best places to find people who know how to "do relationships." That in itself was a significant witness. The foundation folks were surprised to learn of churches that were willing to work for a program they didn't run. Actually, we were thrilled to be relieved from the administrative pressures. This freed us to concentrate our energies on the relationships. The school administrators, many of whom were embattled and defensive, were amazed to find people who wanted to help individuals rather than gain control over school policies. In turn, the churches were surprised to discover that the public schools wanted our help. The project has attracted so much attention in the community that we now find public officials regularly soliciting our advice on social issues—and we're having an effect we never could have gained through angry protest.

The black church and our mostly white church have been meeting for some time now to pray for each other. For years white and black churches in Madison had been talking about the problems of racism, but never to each other. We now have that discussion with our brothers and sisters frequently. But only because we have a relationship with them. We are still a predominantly white church, but we've learned something about responding to our society's problems by the norms of the kingdom rather than the strategies of the world. We have found that it is possible to model a hopeful alternative to injustice, if we act like the church that knows how to live under the kingdom of God in the world.

To cooperate in our mission program not only with churches of different denominations but also with public schools and civic groups has alarmed some who are worried about the purity of the church. They caution us that this partnering would eventually make the walls around the church appear fuzzy and confusing. We hope they're right.

Compromising the Church

Clearly, Jesus didn't come to associate God with those of us who are good, religious or even prophetic in our commitment to the truth. He came to reconcile the lost world to its Creator.

Reconciling is the language of relationships, not problem solving.

In Christ, the Word of God became flesh and lived among us. That same Word dwells among those who frantically try to secure life with power and wealth, and it dwells with those who have neither power nor wealth. This means that the minister of reconciliation is committed to bringing Christ into conflicting interests and causes with such a devotion that he or she will never have the luxury of party allegiances.

As Henri Nouwen told my seminary graduating class, "If after a few years in the ministry you find yourself admired and praised by a loyal following, you have good reason to worry a bit. If you find yourself in the unquestioning support of ideologies, theological schools, or political agendas, you had better wonder just whose minister you are. As well, if you congratulate yourself as the lonely misunderstood prophet of truth, you had better ask yourself if you have missed the point." For the minister of reconciliation has been called to become involved in the confused, complicated, and almost always compromised lives of those with whom God became involved in Jesus Christ.

Materialism, sexism, racism, the abuses of power—how can we be involved in the lives of those broken down by these sins yet not associate with evil? Doesn't our very presence make us guilty by association? Yes, of course it does. Ministry is never clean. This is why Jesus was always in so much trouble with those who maintained religious purity by staying away from sinners. Christ involved himself with sinners in his baptism, in his social life, among his disciples, and, most important, on his cross. By refusing to condemn the adulteress and the cheating tax collector but denouncing those who made a profession out of looking righteous, he confused accepted boundaries between "good" and "bad."

In fulfilling our common calling to be ministers of reconciliation, we must allow our robes of righteousness to become tattered and stained, and possibly even discredited. We must offer the hope of God to those who have made a mess out of life and to those whose righteousness is as filthy rags. This means that the church's mission is not simply a matter of standing for truth, but of standing with those who are in error while testifying to the truth. The walls of the church will always remain fuzzy and compromised if it has seriously engaged the world. But that poses little danger to the holiness of the church, which is defined not by its borders but by its center in Jesus Christ. We do not present ourselves to the world as a distant, pristine alternative culture, as if it were ever possible to return to the good garden. Our models for mission must always come under a strict allegiance to the ministry of Christ—the Word who was made flesh and lived among us.

The church of reconciliation will always find itself between the old and the new, between the way it is and the way it will be, between a hungry, oppressed, unjust world and the slow-coming kingdom of God. As it takes its stand in the midst of how it is, the church hears the deep laments of the world and then faithfully proclaims the God who has come in search of the lost world he loves.

Then the Word is made flesh. Then hope begins to emerge.

The Amen

Now, return with me to the long line of broken lives waiting to receive Communion on Christmas Eve. In holding up the body of Christ, what hope do I give them for next year? Does the broken body promise that things will get better if they can just hang on? In the moment in which my eye catches theirs, do I wink as if to say, "Yes, but soon God will fix it all if you only have faith"? No. Absolutely not.

After receiving the body and blood of Christ, the newly divorced woman will still have to return to her pew alone. The grief-stricken parents will still miss the child they buried last month. And the tired old Alzheimer's victim will still break his wife's heart every time he asks her name.

What I hold up that night is the hope that God has found them. If they can see that, if even for a moment, it is enough. Then everything has changed. Nothing may be different, but those who have realized that they journey with God perceive everything differently. A bit more of the unpredictable light of Christ has broken into the darkness that surrounds them, that surrounds us all. At the holy table of Jesus they've seen God's slow-coming kingdom—not in spite of their brokenness but through it. With that hope, their needy lives are filled with divine significance.

All they can say is "Amen."

Notes

Chapter 1: Telling the Truth

[1]Mircea Eliade, *The Sacred and the Profane* (New York: Harcourt Brace Jovanovich, 1957), 32.

[2]Almost all religious systems have some story—what Eliade calls "myth"—that explains the whys and hows of life. Though they may certainly possess elements of historicity, these myths are true not so much by virtue of their historicity as by the fact that they interpret the existence of the people. They are true to life. The myth provides the model for the people's understanding of both individual and communal life. The importance of a society's institutions, rites of passage, and perspectives on relationships and work can all be traced back to the life-giving interpretation of its primal myths. As people reenact the mythical story, their world becomes sanctified, and their behavior takes on deep significance. Without this significance, their world would not hold together, and the skies would come crashing down.

[3]Jürgen Moltmann, *The Crucified God* (New York: Harper & Row, 1980), 276.

Chapter 2: Remaking or Receiving

[1]The significance of God's uttering "Let there be" is that creation came about by the *Word* of God. It is not the preoccupation of biblical authors to state that this creation came *ex nihilo* (out of nothing). In fact, at times Isaiah uses the term *yatsar* to refer to God's "molding" of creation (43:1,7; 45:18). Whether creation was molded or called into being out of nothingness is not the primary issue in the Old Testament. The more critical concern for biblical authors is that what exists came to us through the Word of the Lord. How he brought about that creation, how long it took, and so forth is a mystery that will be fully understood by God alone. This mystery is beyond the grasp of his creation and, significantly, beside the point of the scriptural narratives.

[2]Alan Jones, *Passion for Pilgrimage: Notes for the Journey Home* (San Francisco: Harper & Row, 1989), 43.

Chapter 3: The Indelible Mark

[1]Paul Jewett, *Man as Male and Female* (Grand Rapids, Mich.: Eerdmans, 1975).
[2]Martin E. Marty, *By Way of Response* (Nashville: Abingdon Press, 1981), 55.
[3]Ibid., 56.

Chapter 4: Chasing the Lie

[1]Gustave Flaubert, *Madame Bovary,* translated by Eleanor Marx-Aveling (New York: Alfred A. Knopf, 1922), 43.
[2]Henrik Ibsen, *Peer Gynt,* translated by Peter Watts (London: Penguin Books, 1966), 157.
[3]Sigmund Freud, "Thoughts for the Times on War and Death," in *Collected Papers,* vol. 4 (New York: Basic Books, 1959), 316-17.
[4]Erich Maria Remarque, *All Quiet on the Western Front,* translated by A. W. Wheen (Boston: Little, Brown, 1929), 185-86.

Chapter 5: Lost and Found

[1]T. S. Eliot, "The Love Song of J. Alfred Prufrock," in *The Modern Poets,* edited by John Brinnin and Bill Read (New York: McGraw-Hill, 1963), 107.
[2]John Barth, *The Floating Opera* (New York: Bantam, 1956), 7.
[3]Reinhold Niebuhr, *Nature and Destiny of Man,* vol 1. (New York: Scribner & Sons, 1941), 239-64.
[4]It is upon a mountain in Moriah that Abraham offers Isaac, upon Mt. Sinai that Moses stands before God, upon Mt. Carmel that Elijah calls fire down from the skies, and upon the Mount of Transfiguration that some of the disciples discover the identity of Jesus as the Son of God. The temple in Jerusalem was built upon Mount Moriah, as if to institutionalize the experience of Abraham and Isaac for the people's worship.
[5]For more information on the "numinous" dimensions of God, see Rudolf Otto, *The Idea of the Holy* (London: Oxford University Press, 1923).

Chapter 6: An Unruly Hope

[1]Gilda Radner, *It's Always Something* (New York: Simon & Schuster, 1989).

Chapter 7: A Family of Grace

[1]For better and worse, families create "the world" in which we develop as children. Our self-understanding, values and arrangement of the world has all been given to us by our families. Like the Creator-God, our parents give us birth, name, identity, sustenance—and they set the boundaries and standards

by which we live. Part of the challenge of maturity is to question the reality of that world, to make necessary adjustments, and to learn to live with both the gifts and the wounds of our early family life.
[2]The New Testament uses many different terms to characterize the church. Among other things, it is called a fellowship, mission, flock, body, and bride. It is called together and it is called out. It is called to proclaim, to witness, and to embody the grace that has created it. A systematic theology of the church could accurately use any one of these images to help us understand the church. I am not trying to provide a theology of the church. But it is important to describe the role of the church in our calling to live with created need. For this purpose, it is most useful to perceive the church as a family, one among many biblical images.
[3]Edwin Friedman, *Generation to Generation* (New York: Guilford Press, 1985), 195ff.
[4]Dietrich Bonhoeffer, *Life Together,* translated by John Doberstein (New York: Harper & Row, 1954), 26-27.
[5]The Protestant church has classically identified the sacraments as only baptism and communion. Roman Catholics list baptism, penance, communion, confirmation, marriage, holy orders and last rites as sacraments. Yet there are many ordinary events that can be accurately referred to as *sacramental* in that they can also provide us with a sacramentlike experience of God's presence.
[6]Cited in Martin E. Marty, *A Cry of Absence: Reflections for the Winter of the Heart* (San Francisco: Harper & Row, 1983), 9-13.
[7]The concept of religious tribes is introduced in Marty, *By Way of Response,* 18ff.
[8]Marty, *A Cry of Absence,* 7.

Chapter 8: Slow Kingdom Coming
[1]Abraham Lincoln, "Second Inaugural Address," quoted in Syndney E. Ahlstrom, *A Religious History of the American People* (New Haven, Conn.: Yale University Press, 1972), 687.
[2]Walter Brueggemann, *Hope within History* (Atlanta: John Knox Press, 1987), 80.
[3]Karl Barth, *Church Dogmatics,* vol. 4, pt. 2, translated by G. W. Bromiley (Edinburgh: T. & T. Clark, 1958), 565.
[4]Simone Weil, *Waiting for God* (New York: G. P. Putnam's Sons, 1951), 69.
[5]Fyodor Dostoyevsky, *The Brothers Karamazov,* translated by Andrew R. MacAndrew (New York: Bantam, 1970), 438.